PEAK DISTRICT TRIGPOINTING WALKS

Hill walking with a point to it!

Keith Stevens &
Peter Whittaker

Published by Sigma Leisure – an imprint of
Sigma Press, 5 Alton Road, Wilmslow, Cheshire SK9 5DY, England.

British Library Cataloguing in Publication Data
A CIP record for this book is available from the British Library.

ISBN: 978-1-85058-835-1

Typesetting and Design by: Sigma Press, Wilmslow, Cheshire.

Cover photograph: Back Tor, Derwent Edge, Walk 8 *(Peter Whittaker)*

Route sketches: the authors

Printed by: Bell & Bain Ltd, Glasgow

Disclaimer: the information in this book is given in good faith and is believed to be correct at the time of publication. No responsibility is accepted by either the author or publisher for errors or omissions, or for any loss or injury howsoever caused. Only you can judge your own fitness, competence and experience. Do not rely solely on sketch maps for navigation: we strongly recommend the use of appropriate Ordnance Survey (or equivalent) maps.

Preface

This is a rambling book with a difference. It describes a completely new walking objective, that is to seek out and log as many as possible of the old Ordnance Survey concrete triangulation pillars; the pastime of 'trigpointing'. You'll need either a GPS receiver or a good compass, preferably both, you'll need to hone your navigational skills, and sometimes you'll have to walk long distances over difficult and unfamiliar terrain.

The pillars are distributed over the whole of the UK, most still standing, some showing the ravages of time, and others destroyed, moved or vandalised. Within the Peak District region there are around 150 to find, enough to keep you occupied for a couple of years and to whet your appetite for more. Can you find 1000 before you hang up your boots? You'll enjoy trying, with the challenge and the sense of achievement adding hugely to the pleasure of your regular walking. And you'll seldom do the same walk twice.

The book provides comprehensive information on the location co-ordinates of the pillars, their history and their triangulation. Their original purpose was to survey and map the country, and we show you how to spot all those pillars that are in sight from the one you've reached, with accurate bearings and distances. Dally a while at the pillar, scan the landscape around you, get to know all the names and geographical features. And when you get back home, build up a log, tick off your finds, assemble your photographs and plan for the next exploration.

Whilst the pillars are the prime objectives, these walks provide a complete experience throughout, with aircraft wrecks, historical landmarks and geological features all included, supported by fascinating background information, history and folklore. A comprehensive route plan for each walk is provided, together with a GPS waypoint and compass bearing summary table, each position recorded by painstaking observations on the ground. And we advise on the special walking safeguards and etiquette that are needed when seeking out some of the pillars that are off the normal walking routes.

You'll find the introduction invaluable. It's a concise and easy to assimilate summary of how the triangulation and mapping was achieved, backed by an explanation of Global Positioning Satellite navigation, the British Grid co-ordinate system, longitude and latitude, bearings and compass points, finding your way by the sun, and computing your horizon distance.

We have provided 20 primary walks, mostly to include two pillars each, in areas as far apart as Holme Moss, Congleton and Matlock. It is suggested that you complete these 20 walks first, before going on to track down the remainder. For those other pillars, we provide advice on how best to group them, where to start from and how to make up a good walk. But we leave most of the planning to you, an essential skill to be learned by the dedicated trigpointer. And importantly, we tell you where to ask permission for access wherever the pillar is on private land.

Whilst a good navigator can enjoy trigpointing with just a compass, we've found a GPS to be a revelation. The hand-held receivers are now smaller, use less power and are more cost-effective than ever. If you can manage a mobile phone, you can master a GPS. And you'll need a good 25 000 to 1 OS map to go with the route sketch maps we provide. Look at the OS map with a new objective; how many of those small blue triangles can you find, the map symbol for the pillars? You'll be astonished at just how many there are and how much walking you're going to have to do to bag them all.

Keith Stevens & Peter Whittaker

Contents

Introduction

All over the country, it now seems that there are hundreds of walkers who set out to complete a new walk each week and 'bag' one or two Ordnance Survey (OS) trig points on the way, recording their condition, OS number and surrounding features. They're only pyramids of concrete, nothing to write home about, but they're part of our heritage and worthy of our patronage. It's not a sport; it's a pastime, an excuse to get out in the fresh air and try out some new ground, with the objective of reaching the pillars adding a new dimension to the walking experience. And back home you can amuse yourself with a computer spreadsheet or a walker's log, recording the visits and assembling the photographs.

Nationwide, there are over 6000 pillars, on average about 8km apart, so there are always plenty to visit in your own area. And once you've bagged all the local trigs and explored dozens of new walks in the process, you'll find yourself dreaming about travelling further afield and perhaps logging 1000 visits before hanging up your boots. Believe it or not, there are walkers out there with more than 3000 visits under their belt. In our case, we'd been walking for years before we leaned on the pillar on top of Shining Tor in the Peak District and asked idly, "I wonder how many there are?"

This book introduces you to the pastime of trigpointing, with 20 challenging walks in the Derbyshire Peak District and surrounding areas. These are for the experienced and dedicated walker, someone willing to take six hours or more and to tackle long distances and difficult terrain. We strongly recommend the use of a Global Positioning Satellite receiver (GPS), both for security and to enhance the walking experience. Programming in an objective and then homing in on the target makes for great walking, even in the most hostile weather conditions. Each walk visits at least one triangulation pillar, but usually more, as well as taking in features of geological and historical interest, including old aircraft crash sites and stone circles. To help, we've included a section on navigation, an essential skill for some of these walks.

Fig 1: The Holme Moss Pillar on Soldier's Lump, north Peak District

The Ordnance Survey pillars

There are over 6000 pillars, and you'll see them on the OS maps as small blue triangles with a central dot. But what are they for, and when and where were they erected? The answer lies 70 years ago, when the formal Ordnance Survey of the UK was begun, with the network of 1.5m (4 ft) high pillars being created from 1936 onwards. Each has a 'spider' on to which can be mounted a theodolite, an accurate compass and telescope. With each pillar being built on a prominent point in the area, with line-of-sight to other nearby pillars, the shape of the country could be determined by measuring the bearing from one pillar to another.

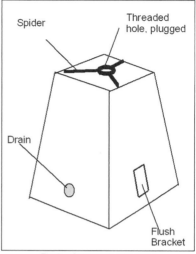

Fig 2 – Schematic of a pillar

As well as the spider, the top of the pillar has a central hole, with a thread to accommodate the secure mounting of a light. When not in use, that hole is plugged, so that most pillars today contain a screwed insert, usually with OS lettering. On the side of the pillar is mounted a metal plate called the Flush Bracket, showing the OS symbol and a number. There are also some holes near the base that act as a drain from the central hole and may also have been used to assist in positioning and levelling the pillar. Finally, under the pillar is a concrete platform buried in the bedrock, extending at least 30cm around the base and up to 1m deep.

The process of surveying is called triangulation, and it has created a network of accurately known reference positions throughout the country, so enabling the creation of the excellent OS maps that greatly enhance our walking experience. They are the basis of the 'British National Grid' system that is so easy to understand and to use.

The first series of pillars to be built was called 'Primaries', covering the country from the most visible locations. There are about 300 of them. After those, the spaces between them were steadily filled with many more 'Secondary' pillars to provide ever more comprehensive triangulation.

Beyond that, individual features at, say, field or street size, could be surveyed from nearby pillars. This finer scale was supported by thousands more Flush Brackets fixed on rocks or buildings that were likely to be long-standing structures.

The triangulation provides only the angles between reference points, not the distances. To measure the scale of the country, it is necessary to know the position of one location very accurately, together with a precise distance to another, also known. This was first attempted in 1784 by laying a series of glass rods along Hounslow Heath, and the same principle was used again in 1936 to begin the great survey. With a single accurate measurement, plus the network of triangula-

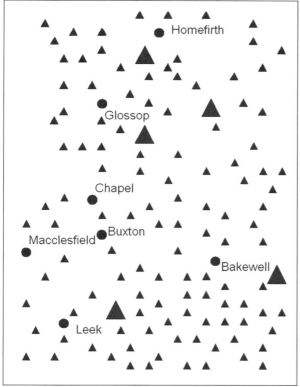

Fig 3 – There are dozens of pillars around the Peak District (the large ones are 'Primaries')

Fig 4 – A Fundamental Bench Mark

tion pillars, the size and shape of the country was determined to within about 20m.

To establish the elevation of a particular spot requires more complex surveying, using another set of reference points called 'Fundamental Bench Marks' (FBM), such as the example near Macclesfield shown in Fig 4. There are around 200 of these small pillars, and some of them top an underground chamber, where the precise benchmark cannot easily be disturbed. They are supported by many thousands of 'Lower Order Benchmarks' engraved on walls, posts and buildings, as well as by bolts set into concrete blocks buried at hundreds of positions around the country.

So the pillars are part of our heritage, even if modern satellite technology has made most of them redundant (but not all, as discussed later), and they are worthy of our respect. At the time, our national survey was the envy of the world, and it set the standard for accuracy and coverage.

Who built them?

The Ordnance Survey gave the task of mapping the country to Captain Martin Hotine, head of the Trigonometrical and Levelling Division. He'd served his time on the North-West Frontier during the First World War, leading from the front. His first decision was that all surveys should be from rigid platforms, not unstable tripods, and he commissioned the construction of the now famous pillars. He was determined to eliminate as much uncertainty as possible by ensuring that any survey from one point was always carried out under exactly the same conditions. The pillars provided an accurate and repeatable location, a fixed height and ensured that the theodolite could always be precisely levelled.

Starting in the south, he worked his teams of men, steadily spreading his pillars all over the country, building them on the spot. There were no helicopters to airlift them into position as would happen now; men and mules had to haul large amounts of material across the most inhospitable terrain. They had to be precise, with the exact weight of cement, sand and chippings being laid down in the handbook. Hotine was certainly a hard taskmaster. It took 12 days in appalling weather to construct the pillar on Cadair Idris, whilst a team of men shivered in the snow for 20 days on Ben Nevis before they could complete their edifice. But there were some compromises. If there was good quality local stone at the site, pillars were occasionally put together as a cemented structure. But they all had the precisely level spider on the top, as well as the flush bracket on one side with the OS number.

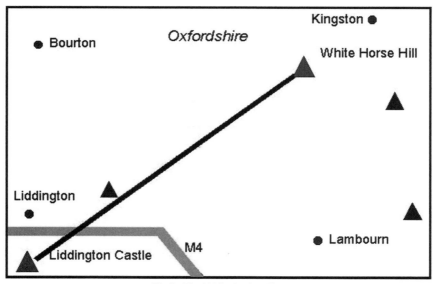

Fig 5 – The Liddington baseline

Hotine established his baseline on The Ridgeway path near Swindon, creating two pillars, one at Liddington Castle and one to the NE on White Horse Hill. He called this the 'Liddington Base Line', and accurately measured its length (11.256km) by using a long tape and a series of very careful steps in a straight line between the two pillars.

From that line he created his first triangle to a third pillar. Using night-time observations to avoid the distortions of the daytime heat-haze, he mounted lights on top of the pillars and focussed his theodolite on those from the other positions. His handbook was very clear; each measurement of the bearing from one pillar to another had to be made 32 times and then averaged, regardless of the huge labour involved. And woe-betide any man caught fiddling the results to get home early!

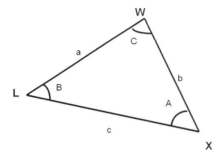

Fig 6 – Basic triangulation

Considering Fig 6, having measured side 'a' very precisely, and taken accurate bearings from 'L' to 'W' and to the new pillar at 'X', angle 'B' is established. Repeating the steps from 'W', taking bearings to 'L' and 'X' gives angle 'C'. After that, angle 'A' is known (180 – A – B), but Hotine would always have it measured to provide more precision. Now sides 'b' and 'c' can be computed by the simple ratios:

$$a/A = b/B = c/C$$

If the position of any one of the pillars (i.e. its longitude/latitude) is accurately determined by taking readings from the stars, then the positions of the other two can be computed. After that, sides 'b' and 'c' could each form a new baseline for two new triangles, a principle that was then repeated until the whole country had been covered.

But there were critics who said that errors would multiply, and that distant positions would become increasingly inaccurate. To prove them wrong, Hotine repeated an accurate tape measurement between two pillars in NE Scotland, as far away from his original baseline as he could get. Using a 30m tape, made in low expansion metal to minimise errors from heating and cooling, it took his team 800 steps and 54 days to determine the true distance between the two Scottish pillars (about 25km apart). The computed distance from all the successive triangulations was only 43cm different, which is less than a two per cent error!

By 1962, all the triangulations had been completed and refined, with the Secondary pillars added to the main batch of Primaries. And from that, the familiar maps that we use today were created. But whilst we are used to seeing the pillars on prominent hills or mountain tops, the majority occupy much less distinguished sites, and in many cases a pillar can be extremely difficult to find, even when your GPS is telling you that you should be standing on it!

For instance, Fig 7 shows the Whiston Hall pillar (in square SJ) buried deep in

Fig 7 – Whiston Hall pillar in square SJ

the hedge and in danger of being totally engulfed. Others turn up in the middle of forests, the plantation having post-dated the pillar and grown to maturity around it.

So how many are left? It's not easy to say, but probably well over 5000. Some have fallen victim to road or housing developments, others to expanding quarries, some to farmers who considered them to be in their way, and others to wanton vandalism. And many of the remaining pillars are showing the ravages of time, with frost and weather erosion chipping away at the fabric. But there are plenty to visit and to log, and we owe it to Captain Hotine to look after them as best we can.

Numbering system

Each of the pillars has a flush bracket with its identifying number. But there is little in the way of system to these numbers, with new ones allocated at different parts of the country as each pillar was erected, so that consecutive numbers can often be hundreds of miles apart. But there are some groups of adjacent pillars in certain areas where the numbers do run currently. Most are four digit figures, from the 1000s to the 9000s, so that with only 6000 pillars being created, there are some numbers unused. In fact, many of the missing numbers can be found on the flush brackets used for lower level positioning, attached to buildings or other permanent structures. Primary pillars usually show only the four-figure number, whereas the vast majority of the Secondary pillars have a letter 'S' preceding the digits.

Finally, some of the later pillars were allocated five-figure numbers, in the range 10 000 to around 12 000, and some of those were replacements for older pillars that had quickly fallen victim to quarries or housing developments. In some cases, the flush bracket and its number were simply re-used for a new pillar. For instance, when the quarry at Bee Low (SK square, north of Buxton) threatened the pillar, it was re-used for a new position at Jodrell Bank (SJ square, mid-Cheshire).

Navigation

Nearly all serious walkers will use Ordnance Survey maps, each drawn up in the familiar British Grid. But the global navigation system is based on longitude and latitude, so it is right to start with an explanation of that.

Longitude/latitude system

Latitude is measured as the angle from the equator; that is a series of parallel 'hoops' around the earth, zero degrees at the equator and 90 degrees at the poles. The UK is positioned between 49 and 61 degrees north, from the Channel Islands to the Shetlands.

Longitude circles are at right angles to the latitude circles, each passing through the two poles. So they are not parallel; they converge as they approach the poles. The most common convention is the system where Greenwich in London is set at zero longitude, so that the UK extends between two degrees east and eight degrees west. 180 degrees west or east is, of course, on the other side of the globe, directly opposite to London.

Before satellite navigation, we relied on the stars, the sun and a compass to establish our position, but even then we had to contend with the complication that magnetic north (to which a compass will point) is not coincident with the true geometric North Pole. From the UK, the magnetic north pole is about **four degrees west of the true north**, so knowing that error allows us to correct for it. But it could have been a lot worse. There is no geological reason why magnetic north should be at the global North Pole, and at times during the long history of the earth it has been nearer the equator than the Pole.

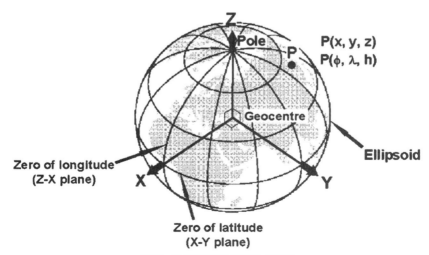

Fig 8 – The longitude/latitude system

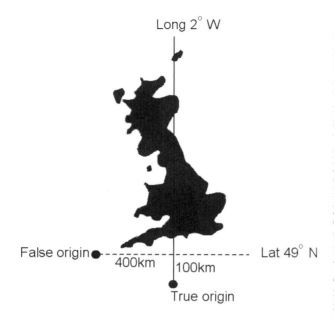

Fig 9 – The origin point to define the British Grid

GPS positioning takes the concept further by establishing angles to orbiting satellites, their position at any one moment being accurately predictable. So when you stand at a point on the earth and your receiver can detect a signal from at least three satellites, your position can be established using triangulation. But importantly, that position is not on the actual earth. It is on an imaginary sphere that is the theoretical best fit for the earth, so that any position measurement is subject to an error, depending on how well the area you are standing on fits to that sphere.

Not only is the earth irregular in shape, it is not actually a true sphere; it is a flattened sphere, so that the best fit is an ellipsoid. So GPS gives you a position on that ellipsoid and, by measuring how far 'out' from it you are, it gives you your elevation from a datum of 'mean sea level'. But both position and height are always approximations.

The most common GPS system is the one established in 1984, the World Geodetic System 1984 (WGS84). It defines an ellipsoid which best fits the whole earth and can even take account of movements in the earth's crust. So, the rule is that when you navigate in longitude/latitude, set your map datum on your GPS to WGS84, as discussed later.

Whilst WGS84 is best for the whole globe, its ellipsoid is not actually the optimum fit for the UK. Much better for us is the 'Airy' ellipsoid called OSGB36, established in 1936 and the source of our triangulation system. It is the basis of the British Grid, as described below, but it is very important to remember that the two ellipsoids are not the same, so that calculation from longitude/latitude to British Grid is very complex.

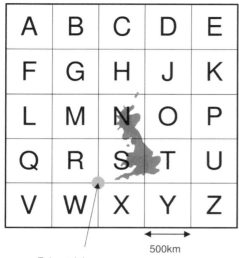

A	B	C	D	E
F	G	H	J	K
L	M	N	O	P
Q	R	S	T	U
V	W	X	Y	Z

←——→
500km

False origin

Fig 10 – The 500km grid squares system around the UK

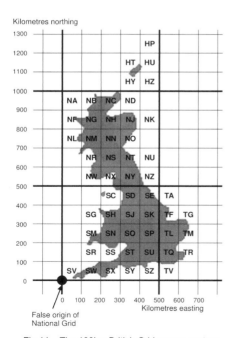

Kilometres northing

Fig 11 – The 100km British Grid square system

False origin of
National Grid

Kilometres easting

The British Grid system

Longitude and latitude readings in degrees, minutes and seconds are quite clumsy to use, unless you are a seasoned traveller and navigator. In contrast, the British Grid system breaks everything down into simple 100km-sided squares, each with designated code letters, so you have a clear vision of where you are in the country.

The system is centred on the longitude line that runs down the spine of the UK that is exactly two degrees west, and on a base that follows the 49 degrees north latitude line. Technically, the origin is at the intersection of those lines, but that would lead to confusing negative and positive co-ordinates for positions in the UK. So the origin (the 'false' origin) is taken at a point 100km north and 400km west of the true origin, off the SW of the UK. From there, any point on the UK land has a unique positive east/north co-ordinate.

For instance, the church marked in the centre of Castleton in the Peak District has the co-ordinates: East 415000, North 382900 (m), That is 415.00km east and 382.90km north of the false origin, to within 100m.

But they are relatively big numbers, and the system can be further simplified by first subdividing the area into a matrix of 500km squares. Here, the system is based on an old military grid square, following the letters of the alphabet (no 'I') as in Fig 10. But on land we are interested in only the H, N, O, S and T squares. Those in turn are divided into the familiar 100km grid squares we see on the OS maps, as in Fig 11.

Each major square is divided into 25 smaller squares and lettered from A to Z (again without the 'I') from top left to bottom right. In the Peak District, we are concerned mostly with the NW corner of square SK.

Now the co-ordinates are measured from the SW corner of the square which you are in, such that the church in Castleton becomes:

SK 15000, 82900, where the convention is always to quote the easting first.

The four corners of the square are:

SW – SK 00000, 00000
NW – SK 00000, 99999
NE – SK 99999, 99999
SE – SK 99999, 00000

And, for instance, the NE corner of square SK will be coincident with the SW corner of square TA, at TA 00000, 00000.

There is one important issue to understand. The earth's surface is curved, but the British Grid is flat. Try wrapping a flat piece of paper round a ball, and wrinkles at the edges are inevitable. The details are complex, but for most walking purposes the errors produced by this compromise are small, so that the British Grid system is always to be recommended for the rambler.

Also, it should be noted that only one vertical line on the grid runs true north-south, that is the **longitude two degrees west** line on which the grid is centred (called the 'central meridian'), along the western edges of squares NU, NZ, SE, SK, SP, SU and SZ. On that line, Grid North and True North coincide. But no other vertical line in the grid follows a true longitude line because the squares are 'square' and do not converge as they run north. For instance, the eastern edge of square SK (100km to the **east** of the central meridian), if projected Grid North, will miss the geographic North Pole by 100km to the east. In terms of angle, it means that, on that grid line, True North is near **one degree west** of Grid North. Conversely, 100km to the **west** of the central meridian, on the west edge of square SJ, True North is **one degree east** of Grid North. If you look on your OS maps you will see an indication of True North on the top edge.

So that's True North, Magnetic North and Grid North to confuse you! But don't despair; your GPS will always get you there. Just remember to set the position format as 'British Grid' and the map datum as 'Ordnance Survey GB'; do not use longitude/latitude with OS, or British Grid with WGS84. A GPS can also be set to correct for the True North/Magnetic North variation, provided that you know the degrees offset for your location.

In this book, we use British Grid co-ordinates throughout, and it is our experience that the OS pillars are usually within five metres of where you'd expect them from the stated co-ordinates. This is due to the uncertainty of your GPS rather than any error in the pillar location (unless someone has moved it). For most other features on a map, there will be greater errors in their survey position, so that an uncertainty nearing 20m is more likely.

Walker's hand-held GPS

For the walker, a hand-held GPS comes as a huge revelation. It brings so much more than does a traditional compass, and can greatly add to the enjoyment of the walk. Basically, it receives signals from the orbiting satellites, and when it has locked on to sufficient numbers (three is a minimum), it can display your position and height. Then, by defining a 'waypoint' with specific co-ordinates, you can select that as a 'go-to' target and the receiver will display the direction to follow and the distance to your objective.

Fig 12 – Typical hand-held GPS

The equipment also allows you to plot a 'route', that is a sequence of waypoints, so that you can pre-programme the walk, the receiver automatically moving on to point to the next waypoint as you prog-

ress. It will compute your distance walked, your average speed, your time actually moving, your total time out, and allow you to 'mark' a spot as you walk. This last facility is useful for recording the exact co-ordinates of interesting features that you might come across and, not least, the starting point of your walk. This provides a ready answer to the most common question from your walking colleagues; "How far is it back to the car?"

As well as the satellites, there are some ground-based transmitters that have precisely known positions. They are called 'active stations', but they are not usually relevant to the rambler. Finally, the positions of some of the old pillars have been re-measured more accuracy, and are recorded in the system as 'passive stations'. There are some such pillars in the Peak District.

One point to consider is batteries. A GPS consumes more power than do most portable devices, so it is best to use rechargeables, and nowadays the best batteries will far outlive your longest walks. Also remember that a GPS tells you in what direction and how far is your target destination; it cannot tell you if there is a sheer cliff or a deep lake in the line of your path!

Compass bearings

It is easy to take the old compass for granted, but a reminder of the principles will not go amiss. Starting with north, the direction you take, i.e. the 'bearing', is measured in degrees, rotating clockwise. So north is zero, east is 90 deg, south is 180 deg and west is 270 deg. It is a simpler concept, once you get to know it, than the compass point system. That relies on successively halving the angle between two directions to describe a new direction.

For instance, half way between north (N) and east (E) is north-east (NE). Half way between N and NE is NNE (meaning north of north-east). And half way between N and NNE is NNNE (meaning north of north-north-east). But half way between NNE and NE is ENNE (meaning east of north-north-east). And so on, until your brain hurts!

To help, here in Table 1 is a summary of the main compass point bearings.

Using a compass to reach a remote objective

Prior to the emergence of the GPS, a compass and a map had been the walker's primary means of navigation. Some of the walks in this book require accurate navigation, walking across featureless moor to an objective that might be 1km distant. With a GPS, it is a straightforward task to programme in the co-ordinates and to follow the indi-

Direction	Bearing (deg)	Direction	Bearing (deg)
N	0 (and 360)	S	180
NNNE	11	SSSW	191
NNE	23	SSW	203
ENNE	34	WSSW	214
NE	45	SW	225
NENE	56	SWSW	236
ENE	68	WSW	248
EENE	79	WWSW	259
E	90	W	270
EESE	101	WWNW	281
ESE	113	WNW	293
SESE	124	NWNW	304
SE	135	NW	315
ESSE	146	WNNW	326
SSE	158	NNW	338
SSSE	169	NNNW	349

Table 1

cated direction. But with just a compass and a map, it's more tricky.

The first task is to establish a bearing to the objective, so your present position on the map must be known. Place the compass on the map, with the centre on your present position. Then rotate the map until the Grid North lines align with the indicated north on the compass. Finally, read off the angular bearing to the objective, using a ruler to help if required, as in Fig 13. In that example, with the compass aligned to Grid North, the angle (bearing) between your position 'P' and your objective is 100 deg. You would then walk with the compass in front of you, keeping to that bearing as far as the terrain allows. If you have an electronic compass, with a digital read-out, then all the better.

Fortunately, because the location of the walks in this book is near the central meridian of the grid system, True North is so close to Grid North as to make no practical difference. But the compass shown in Fig 13 is, in fact, pointing to Magnetic North, not True North. At the time of writing this book, that means an error of about four degrees, Magnetic North being west of True North. Hence, the more accurate bearing to the objective is

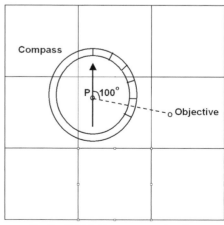

Fig 13 – Establishing a compass bearing

100 + 4 = 104 deg. Always add on the four degrees, even when the objective is to the west. For instance, an indicated SW bearing of 225 deg becomes 229 deg. To put that in perspective, walking 1km with an error of 4 deg would mean missing the objective by 70m.

On the ground, when the bearing as been established from your map, it may be possible to locate the objective in the distance. Then it becomes a straightforward task to keep it in sight and walk towards it. But in poor weather, with rain and cloud, visibility may be as low as 50m. In that case, it is necessary to progress carefully in a series of steps, 'marking' a visible point on the ground (a rock, a patch of heather, etc) that is on the correct bearing, and walking to it. Then the process is repeated to another 'mark', and so on to the objective. With two walkers, one can move forward (keeping in sight!) and act as the mark, the second then following. We call that the 'walk to' method, and it is referred to in some of the walks. If the objective is an OS pillar, perhaps 1km distant across the moor, not correcting for Magnetic North could well mean that you'll miss it by a distance greater than your visibility.

There is no doubt, therefore, that a GPS brings a significant advantage in navigation. But some walkers may like to test their skills to the limit, finding the remote pillars with just a compass, even in poor weather. In this book, we provide the important (true) bearings for any critical parts of a walk, so there is no need to establish them on the ground. Wrestling with a large OS map, a compass and a ruler, in the wind and rain, can test even the most dedicated walker's forbearance!

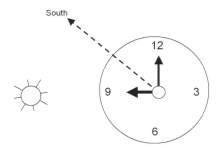

Fig 14 – Finding south with your watch.

Navigation by your watch

The first requirement is that you can see the sun. After that it's easy. Simply point the hour hand of your watch at the sun, and then south is halfway between the hour hand and the '12' on your dial. That's assuming it's Greenwich Mean Time (GMT); if it's British Summer Time (BST), then south is half way between the hour hand and the '1' on your dial.

For instance, at 6am GMT, the sun will be due east. If you point the hour hand at that, the '12' will be opposite, due west. And halfway is, obviously, due south. The example in Fig 14 is for 9am GMT.

Time		Direction of sun
GMT	BST	
6am	7am	E
9am	10am	SE
12 noon	1pm	S
3pm	4pm	SW
6pm	7pm	W

An easy table to remember

Your horizon

How far is the horizon from a given elevation? It's a relevant question when asking whether you might be able to see another pillar from the one you're standing by, even assuming there are no hills in your line-of-sight.

The calculation is simple enough, relying on good old Pythagoras and his right-angled triangle.

R is the radius of the earth (6400km, 4000 miles), X is your height above sea level and H is the distance you can see to a point at sea level.

$R^2 + H^2 = (R + X)^2$, and after a bit of maths, you can conclude that:

$H = 3578\sqrt{X}$, when in metres

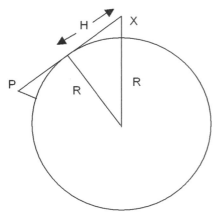

Fig 15 – The horizon problem

The graph in Fig 16 shows, for instance, that at an elevation of 600m (the highest trig point in the Peak District) it's possible to see a theoretical 88km (55 miles) to sea level, assuming a clear day and no obstructions. But if you look at the picture in Fig 15 you'll see that, if there was another peak 600m high 88km beyond your horizon (at position 'P' in Fig 15), then theoretically you'd be able to see the top of it, at a total distance of 176km. So, from the Shining Tor pillar near Buxton (550m elevation), you should be able to see the top of Snowdon (1085m), some 140km away. But even on the clearest day it would be so small that you'd struggle to recognise it.

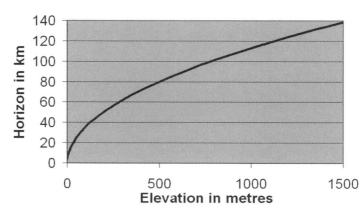

Fig 16 – Horizon as a function of your elevation

The Peak District Pillars

The full and completely accurate list of UK pillars is not easy to come by, with some of the OS records being incomplete or lost in the mists of time. But we are interested primarily in the Peak District pillars, and we believe that the list of around 130 tabled below covers the region. In that respect, we define the Peak District as a region of popular

Fig 17 – Not every pillar remains intact. This is the forlorn pillar on Lantern Pike, pulled over by vandals.

walking embracing an area from the moors east of Oldham in the north, to Ashbourne in the south. To the west, we include the areas just east of Congleton and Macclesfield, and to the east as far as the moors that lie to the west of Chesterfield and Sheffield.

Those pillars known to be missing are highlighted as 'MIS', those moved or toppled over as 'MOV'. Passive station (PS) pillars and Primaries (PRIM) are also indicated. The majority are in British Grid square SK, with just a few in SJ and SE, most of the pillars remaining in position and intact. Many are on private property, and even with the latest Open Access legislation (CROW), on the ground it is never easy to decide on your rights. So we have selected only those pillars for the 20 main walks that have unambiguous public access.

At the end of the section on the walks there is a discussion about most of the other pillars, with indications on their access, where to ask permission and on the attractions (or otherwise) of the area for good walking. In many cases, we indicate further walks to take in groups of those pillars.

Table 2a – The SE Peak District pillars

Name	East	North	Ht (m)	Name	East	North	Ht (m)	Name	East	North	Ht (m)
Alphin Pike	00296	02817	469	Holme Moss (PRIM)	07816	04684	582	South Nab	15629	00319	461
Dead Edge End	12445	01728	500	Saddleworth	02076	06964	455	Standedge	01236	10415	449
Featherbed Moss	04643	01169	541	Snailsden	13198	03311	476	West Nab	07644	08792	501

Table 2b – The SJ Peak District pillars

Name	East	North	Ht (m)	Name	East	North	Ht (m)	Name	East	North	Ht (m)
Blakelow	93420	72395	292	High Bent	91559	59319	336	Shining Tor	99463	73739	559
Cobden Edge	98675	87249	328	Kerridge Hill	94245	75948	314	Shutlingsloe	97645	69574	506
Croker Hill	93372	67696	404	Kniveden Reservoir	99923	56069	266	Sponds Hill	97001	80294	411
Dunwood	95148	55116	231	Marple Ridge	96215	87266	203	The Cloud	90469	63659	344
Gun	97006	61515	386	Mow Cop	85841	57540	336	The Common	95344	57128	213
Hilly Field	97819	57877	194	Nab Head	94007	78837	285				

Table 2c – The SK Peak District pillars

Name	East	North	Ht (m)	Name	East	North	Ht (m)	Name	East	North	Ht (m)
Abney Moor	18043	79421	417	Flask Edge	28492	78842	395	Moor Top (PS)	02964	55303	401
Aleck Low	17502	59475	394	Grange Hill	31539	73609	299	Musden Low	11832	50080	360
Alport Heights (PRIM)	30560	51583	315	Grindon Moor	07153	55089	374	Noton Barn	21667	66169	209
Axe Edge	03502	70613	552	Harborough Rocks	24264	55337	379	Oaker Hill	27120	61303	194
Back Tor	19763	90991	538	Hardings Booth	07203	63937	361	Outer Edge	17703	96973	542
Bank Top	11802	60064	266	Harland S (PRIM & PS)	30088	68157	367	Ox Stones	28021	83134	420
Batemans Plantation	26759	55587	358	Harry Hut	04477	90771	441	Parsley Hay Farm	14594	64229	374
Bee Low (MIS)	09244	79147	410	Hasker Farm	26458	52516	281	Revidge	07739	59910	400
Birchen Edge	27825	73093	310	Hawks Low	16972	57028	382	Reynards	15107	52677	369
Black Edge	06254	77006	507	High Low	15571	67700	312	Ringinglow	29957	83652	321
Black Heath	05021	49866	381	High Neb	22816	85344	458	Rod Moor	26268	88413	384
Blacka Plantation	28995	81251	295	High Rake (MOV)	20881	73402	392	Sheen Hill	11055	62539	380
Blackstones Low	21000	55420	296	High Wheeldon	10037	66111	422	Sir William Hill	21538	77891	429
Blake Mere (PRIM)	04134	60999	489	Higher Shelf Stones	08894	94787	621	Slipper Low	22701	56897	368
Blakelow Hill	25454	59395	367	Hill House	05169	58571	425	Soles Hill	09794	52505	355
Bole Hill	18403	67589	356	Hind Low (MIS)	08087	68960	449	Sough Top	13330	70896	439
Bradnop	03842	54265	405	Hoftens Cross	07629	47766	363	Stanage Edge	25094	83017	457
Bradwell Moor	13179	80133	471	Hollinsclough Moor	05531	65838	424	The Edge (PRIM)	07698	89370	625
Brown Knoll	08369	85129	560	Hopping Top	20977	62718	272	The Mountain	26722	49270	243
Burbage Edge	02960	73247	500	Ipstones	01567	50069	273	The Roaches	00107	63891	506
Calton Pastures	23779	68174	290	Kinder Low	07904	87059	633	Tittesworth Farm	00403	58328	238
Chinley Churn	03549	83633	451	Kirk Edge	27723	92947	396	Totley	30344	79652	234
Cliff Top	13631	48153	316	Ladder Hill	02772	78867	406	Wardlow	17851	73972	371
Cock Hill	05931	96189	427	Lantern Pike (MOV)	02375	87961	359	Weaver Hill (PRIM)	09454	46389	371
Corbar Hill	05138	74298	437	Lean Low	14956	62235	393	West End Moor	12878	93255	503
Cown Edge Rocks (MIS)	02156	92038	411	Long Rake	18363	64158	330	Wetton Low	11223	54743	323
Ecton Hill	09979	57998	370	Madge Hill	21863	49595	298	Wheston	13841	76565	381
Edale Moor	12927	87809	590	Mam Tor	12769	83612	517	White Edge	26378	75855	365
Elton Common	22069	60220	330	Margery (PRIM))	18911	95695	546	Whitwell Moor	24972	97237	359
Emlin Ridge	23987	93364	385	Martins Low	07112	51986	295	Wibben Hill	18374	52247	250
Fairfield	07770	74422	355	Masson Hill (MIS)	28603	58670	339	Winhill Pike	18678	85093	463
Fallinge	27612	65478	327	Milk Hill	09350	49560	286	Wolfscote Hill	13705	58323	388
Farley	30053	26072	302	Moor Plantations	24496	62906	324	Wormhill	10721	75621	403

The walks

For each of the twenty primary walks, we've indicated the preferred start and parking facilities, the route and its degree of difficulty, including the distance, total ascent and estimated walking time, which usually implies an average speed of about two miles/hour (3.2km/hour). The 38 pillars are discussed in terms of access, location and condition, as well as the line-of-sight and bearing to each of the nearby pillars. Where possible, we also describe interesting geographical and historical features around the walk to make the day a complete experience. In the section on 'Access to other pillars', ideas for 25 more walks are suggested to take in a further 46 pillars. Finally, information is also given in that section on 'drive bys' how best to visit the remaining 50 pillars and other OS survey points, usually as a 'drive-by' and short walk to each one.

We suggest the use of a GPS, and provide all the important waypoints to help you keep to the route. And for those walkers who prefer a compass, we give the accurate bearings needed to negotiate the more difficult sections of the walks. This particularly applies when moving off established paths across open-access land, areas that bring difficult walking and challenge your navigation skills. A compass is also needed when reaching each pillar objective, so that all the nearby pillars that surround the position can be identified. And a pair of binoculars will help to pick them out.

All the walks are on established rights of way, open-access areas or on unmarked routes that are clearly well-used and accepted concessionary paths on the ground. There is some road walking, mostly on quiet lanes. With the advent of 'CROW' ('Countryside and Rights of Way' Act), some of the walks venture on to newly opened land where there are, as yet, no stiles and few gates. For those areas, we ensure that the route enters and leaves the Open Access area through practical access points. If an area is Open Access, but with some restrictions, we provide the relevant information in the walk description. Often, on Open Access grouse moor, those restrictions will forbid dogs at certain times of the year.

A useful website to consult in regard to access rights and restrictions is: http://cms.countrysideaccess.gov.uk.

Route sketches

Each walk has a hand-drawn route sketch, produced by painstaking observations on the ground and by using a GPS to record a sequence of waypoints and elevations that then define the route and its height profile. Whilst every effort has been made to ensure that the sketches are a good representation of the walks and the surrounding key points, they cannot be used as your sole walking guide. The scale is approximate and the sketches are in no way geographically accurate. So it is imperative that you take with you a good quality Ordnance Survey map, preferably with a 25 000 to 1 scale, and that time is spent before the walk matching the route to the official map.

Where possible, we have added key grid-references for critical points on the walk, as determined with a GPS on the ground, and we include a summary table of waypoints at the end of each walk. It is suggested that a copy of that table be taken on the walk, or better still that the sequence of waypoints is programmed into a GPS as a 'route'. The waypoints determined on the ground are each rounded to the nearest 10m, but the co-ordinates for the pillars are those taken from OS and other records, quoted to within one metre. We have found them to be reassuringly precise.

The routes can be followed without a GPS, but a quality OS map and good map-reading skills would then be essential. On a 25 000 to 1 map (1km squares being 40mm by 40mm), by using a 1mm-squared graticule overlay (available in outdoor pursuit shops), it is possible to resolve a position to within 25m. When traversing open moorland, aiming for a distant waypoint, without the GPS it would be necessary to make accurate use of a compass, including a correction for the Magnetic North error. The compass bearings required to negotiate critical parts of the walks are also provided in the summary tables.

Units of distance

The walks are described in kilometres (km) and metres (m), with some conversions to miles and feet where it is helpful. OS maps are laid out in 1km squares, and the British Grid system is based on metres, so for walks that make repeated use of a GPS and British Grid co-ordinates it is best to employ the metric system. When judging walking distances, one yard and one metre can be regarded as equivalent, and 1.6km = 1 mile. So a 10 mile walk is 16km.

Safety

Any walk can bring hazards, even on well-established paths. But some of the routes are across open moor, with challenging terrain. Be extra cautious, don't rush, and carefully judge the ground in front. Peat moor presents particular hazards, as running water can undercut the surface, leaving fragile overhangs or bridges. Steep-sided peat groughs are a major slip hazard. Manoeuvre around them rather than trying to cross them; the extra distance is worth it.

Do not walk alone. On some of the walks, particularly in less than ideal weather, you may not meet any other ramblers, so an accident could leave you in serious difficulty. Always keep a close track on your map position, and have in mind the shortest route to safety should the weather close in. In an emergency, use your mobile phone (signal permitting) to dial 999, asking for 'mountain rescue'. But remember that it is for emergencies only, not to help find your way if you are lost. Finally, make sure you have enough daylight to complete the walk, with a bit to spare for unforeseen delays.

Country code

Respect the country code at all times; take your litter home, close gates, don't abuse fences or walls, keep to the path wherever possible and do not alarm grazing stock or free-range birds, especially with dogs. In particular, do not blatantly trespass in pursuit of a pillar that is on private land. Always ask permission; most farmers and landowners will gladly comply, often expressing an interest in what you are doing and in the history of the pillars. Many are quite proud of their own pillar and take time to paint it, plough carefully around it and prevent it being overgrown.

Some trig-points may be buried in hedges. If you have permission for the visit, be very circumspect in your efforts to uncover the pillar. Clearing of brambles and nettles is not usually a problem, but do not presume to cut away large pieces of hedging to clear your access.

Be cautious of farming stock. On established paths, farmers have certain obligations, for instance not to endanger walkers with unpredictable animals such as a lone bull. But when walking on private land, with permission, be aware that those same obligations will not apply. Some of the walks are across long stretches of open peat and heather moor. In very dry weather, the risk of fire is serious; be extra vigilant, don't smoke.

Equipment

We suggest the following equipment is essential.

♦ Good sized rucksack with adequate space for all your walking provisions.

♦ Good quality walking boots, with spare socks. Also take spats and waterproof over-trousers for wet conditions.

♦ Waterproof and windproof jacket, preferably with a hood, and a fleece for winter conditions.

♦ In hot summer conditions, a hat for head protection.

♦ In winter conditions, with the possibility of blowing snow, a balaclava to protect your face. Also, good quality gloves and at least one walking pole.

♦ Spare clothing, such as shirt and underwear, against a fall into water or deep snow.

♦ Adequate food, and particularly water. Beware of dehydration during hot summer conditions.

♦ First-aid kit.

♦ Survival bag for emergency use.

♦ Good maps, a clear route plan, your GPS, fully charged, a compass and a mobile phone.

♦ Whistle and torch.

♦ Inform friends or family where you are planning to walk and your likely return time.

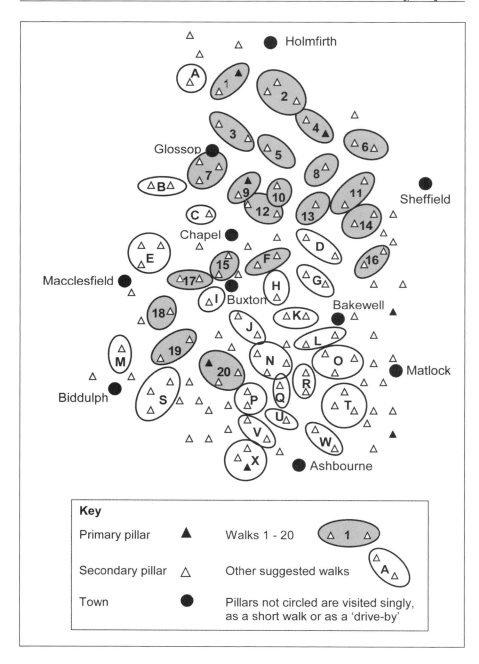

Locations of the walks

The sketch map shows the location of the 20 main walks, mostly in the north of the Peak District. The remaining walks, denoted A to X, are described in the section Access to other Peak District pillars.

Walk grading

The walks are graded as follows:

Easy: On established paths, with a relatively short distance and modest total ascent.

Moderate: On established paths, around 14km distance and up to a 500m total ascent.

Strenuous: Generally longer than 16km, and/or with greater than a 500m total ascent, but mostly using established paths.

Difficult: Involving off-path walking across difficult terrain, such as peat bog, wet grass moor or deep heather moor. Distance and ascent may be in the 'moderate' category, but a 'difficult' walk will also be 'strenuous'.

Route	➔	Rocky edge	
Road		Wooded area	
Marsh/wet land	~ ~ ~	Building	■
No obvious path	●●●●●●●●●➤	Church or Chapel	✦
Other path	- - - - - - - -	Cairn	★
Point of interest	●	Lake or Reservoir	
Triangulation pillar	▲	River or stream	
Triangulation pillar toppled or destroyed	△	Ruin	◣
Track or drive	- - - - - - -	Cemetery	+
Dam	▬▬▬	Bridge	⌒
Rock formation	◢	Railway line	+++++++
Rocky outcrop		Arial or mast	⊺
Quarry		Summit	✹

Key to walk route sketches

Walk 1 – Featherbed Moss and Holme Moss

Start: At Crowden car park opposite Torside reservoir – Map reference SK 07250 99270

Distance: 16km (10.0 miles)

Total ascent: 560m (1820 ft)

Estimated time: 5.5 hours

Grading: Difficult; not recommended when deep snow is lying

OS map: Explorer map OL 1 The Peak District – Dark Peak area

The route

The route follows the Pennine Way NW, makes an excursion across the moor to the Featherbed Moss pillar, before returning to the Pennine Way and continuing to the Holme Moss Pillar. The return leg is south along a moorland path over White Low and Hey Moss.

The height profile shows a steady start, a stiff climb, then relatively level walking across the Featherbed Moss moor and up to the Holme Moss pillar. The route back is steadily downhill, but with a very steep final descent.

The walk

Exit the car park from the west corner, passing the information boards and walking through the wooded area to the facility block at Crowden campsite. Turn right there (north), following the walled track for 300m, and then turning left (west) at the T-junction, signposted 'Pennine Way'. The track crosses Crowden Great Brook and a dyke, part of the complex catchment system that channels water into the Longdendale valley reservoirs to the south.

From the other side of the brook, the track continues west, reaching a signpost at SK 06870 99070, again identifying the Pennine Way. Turning right there (NNW), follow the field path for 400m to a gate at SK 06720 99470. There, another path leaves uphill towards the Lad's Leap escarpment. Although it proceeds in the right direction, that path is not a viable route to the Featherbed Moss pillar. After the gate, continue north on the Pennine Way, with a small copse of trees on your right. As the path emerges into the open, the view to the fore expands, the valley carrying the Crowden Great Brook and the northerly leg of the route stretching ahead.

Having passed below Black Tor, at SE 06290 00400 the route crosses a stream, following a well-walked path that climbs steadily below Rakes Rocks and onwards to another stream, called Oaken Clough. There, at SE 05850 00940, the

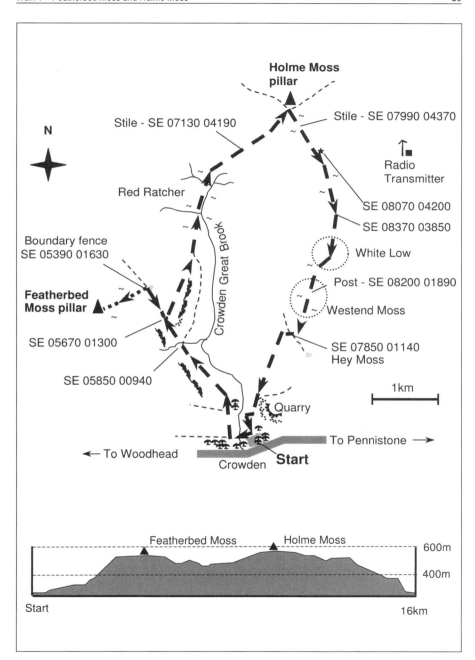

Holme Moss pillar

Stile - SE 07130 04190

Stile - SE 07990 04370

N

Radio Transmitter

Red Ratcher

SE 08070 04200

SE 08370 03850

Crowden Great Brook

Boundary fence
SE 05390 01630

White Low

Featherbed Moss pillar

Post - SE 08200 01890

Westend Moss

SE 05670 01300

SE 07850 01140
Hey Moss

SE 05850 00940

1km

Quarry

To Pennistone →

← To Woodhead

Crowden **Start**

Featherbed Moss   Holme Moss

600m

400m

Start

16km

path reaches a fork. Take the left path (NNW), ascending a set of stone steps, immediately after crossing the clough. After a stiff climb to the edge above Ladlow Rocks, at SE 05670 01300 the path divides again, the Pennine Way (the route to be followed later) veering NNE. To reach the Featherbed Moss pillar requires a detour, taking the left fork to the NW, the path following a wide gully for 400m to a stile in the county boundary fence at SE 05390 01630.

From the stile, leave the path, taking a 240 deg bearing (true) across the peat moor, setting the GPS objective as SE 04643 01169 (the pillar) and following any of the faint paths that have been created by walkers. Note that, on some maps, the pillar is shown as being on the county boundary line, but on the ground the boundary fence runs well to its east. With a compass only, and no GPS, and when there is poor visibility, finding the pillar will be a serious challenge. It's on the highest point, but the 'walk to' method, as described in the Introduction, will improve your chances. If you become disorientated, give up the search and set a return course NE. It will lead either to the boundary fence (then turn left) or the path (then turn right).

Featherbed Moss pillar is completely intact, with all its original features, including the OS screwed insert in the centre of the spider. But the peat that once surrounded the base has been eroded away, exposing the concrete platform and the bedrock below.

The pillar details are:

Position: SE 04643 01169
Flush bracket No: S2628
Height: 541m (1758 ft)
Horizon: 83km (52 miles)
Built: June 1939
Historic use: Secondary
Current use: None
Condition: Fair

Featherbed Moss pillar

There is line-of-sight to 10 local pillars from Featherbed Moss, so that it is not one of the highest visibility sites. Views round from SW to the north are restricted by the relatively flat expanse of the moor itself. For instance, Saddleworth Moor, only 6km to the NW, is not in sight.

Leaving the pillar, retrace the route back to the stile in the boundary fence and then on to the edge above Ladlow Rocks (SE 05670 01300). The precise bearing from the pillar to the stile is 60 deg (NE). Turn left at Ladlow Rocks (NNE) and follow the Pennine Way along the edge. It's a well-worn path, generally dry, but scattered with loose rocks that can make for precarious walking.

Pillar	Distance	Direction
Holme Moss (Primary)	4.7km	NE (041 deg)
Dead Edge End	7.8km	E (086 deg)
South Nab	11.0km	E (094 deg)
Outer Edge	13.7km	ESE (108 deg)
Margery Hill (Primary)	15.3km	ESE (111 deg)
Higher Shelf Stones	7.7km	ESSE (146 deg)
The Edge (Primary) *	12.2km	SSSE (165 deg)
Harry Hut	10.4km	S (180 deg)
Cown Edge Rocks **	9.5km	SSSW (195 deg)
Cobden Edge	15.1km	SSW (203deg)

* The visibility to this pillar is marginal; ** Pillar missing

At around SE 06100 02600 the path descends to the level of the Crowden Great Brook in the bottom of the valley. Then, as it accompanies the brook NNE past Red Ratcher, it encounters several streams and marshy areas, both of which can create walking hazards, particularly in frosty conditions. The best policy through the marshy areas is to keep as close as possible to the brook itself. From SE 06230 03190 the path is paved, with good walking NE over Grain Moss and Dun Hill for the next 1.1km. At SE 07130 04190 the path crosses a stile in another county boundary fence. On the other side, the paved section continues up to a point 600m from the Holme Moss pillar, where it reverts to a gritstone and peat path. Approaching within 100m of the pillar, more paving takes the path over the final expanse of peat moor.

Since the pillar was erected in 1936, it's probable that at least a quarter of a million walkers have passed along this section of the Pennine Way, many pausing at the site for rest and refreshment. Their influence on erosion is plain to see from the pillar itself, the base of the pyramid (which was level with the peat ground when it was erected) now standing more than a metre higher, with the concrete foundations having been buttressed with stones and a paving base. Because of its popularity and the extremes of the weather, the entire area around the pillar has lost 2cm (about an inch) of peat every year for the last 70 years, the heather and grass unable to survive the relentless footfall, and the rain doing the rest.

Despite the support, the pillar is leaning, but otherwise it remains intact. It is a Primary pillar (with no 'S' before the flush bracket number), one of the first 300 to be erected, so it formed part of the initial triangulation network.

The pillar details are:

Position: SE 07816 04684
Flush bracket No: 2958
Height: 582m (1891 ft)
Horizon: 86km (54 miles)
Built: Mid 1936
Historic use: Primary
Current use: None
Condition: Fair

Holme Moss pillar

As with the Featherbed Moss pillar, there is line-of-sight to just 11 local pillars, but the visibility to the NW is improved, so that Standedge and Moss Moor come into view. Again, it is the flat-topped moorland site that restricts the visibility in several directions, and many of the Secondary pillars visited in the other walks described in this book have much better all-round views.

Pillar	Distance	Direction
Snailsden *	5.6km	EESE (104 deg)
Dead Edge End *	5.5km	SESE (122 deg)
Outer Edge	12.5km	SESE (128 deg)
Margery Hill (Primary)	14.2km	SESE (129 deg)
Higher Shelf Stones	10.0km	SSSE (173 deg)
The Edge (Primary)	12.6km	S (180 deg)
Harry Hut	14.3km	SSSW (193 deg)
Featherbed Moss	4.7km	SW (221 deg)
Standedge	8.7km	NW (311 deg)
Moss Moor	12.2km	NW (314 deg)
Cupwith Hill	10.4km	NNW (334 deg)

* The visibility to these pillars is marginal

Taking a more distant perspective reveals that it has good views to four other Primaries, Rivington, by the Winter Hill TV transmitter, Boulsworth, near Burnley, Rombalds Moor, just south of Ilkley, and Upton Beacon, south of Pontefract in Yorkshire. Whilst, in clear weather, you'll be able to stand by the pillar and identify the local peaks, maybe even resolving the pillars themselves with binoculars, it won't be easy to identify the very distant Primary positions. As explained in the Introduction, Hotine had his surveyors work at night, measuring the bearing angles to lights that were positioned on the pillars that were being viewed, even at distances up to 50km.

From Holme Moss pillar, head in a SSE direction (138 deg bearing) across 400m of peat and gritstone to a fence stile at SE 07990 04370. There is no clear path to follow, so that if visibility is poor, it's important to set the target GPS waypoint or to make accurate use of your compass. From there, the route uses a path that has been established by walkers over the years. It is preferred over the right of way path, shown on most of the maps, which runs parallel and around 100m to the east. Across the wet, grassy moor, the path is sometimes unclear, but the route follows a chain of small cairns and marker posts, most of which have been identified with a map reference, as well as other points between them.

After the fence stile, the first cairn is 200m SSE at SE 08070 04200. From this point onwards (assuming a clear day), there are views eastwards to the impressive Holme Moss radio transmitter, one of the most powerful in the country. The original aerial was erected in 1951, that being demolished and replaced by the current mast in 1984. It stands 228m high, supported by massive steel guy ropes, at an elevation of 530m, making it one of the highest masts in the country. It currently broadcasts BBC National FM, Radio GMR and Radio Sheffield, in addition to digital radio, but never TV.

From the cairn at SE 08070 04200, the path SE across Tooleyshaw Moss is mainly through groughs and across peat bogs. After 500m, at SE 08370 03850, where the route veers to the SSE, the ground changes to wet grass moor, so that the walking is more straightforward. The next waypoint, 900m SSE (bearing 174 deg), is a marker post at SE 08540 02990 on Tooleyshaw Moor, the open moor-

Quarry spoil

land walking then continuing for another 800m to White Low. The waypoint there is SE 08440 02250, the path then turning SSW for 400m and passing a marker post at SE 08200 01890 as it crosses Westend Moss. From there, the path drops steadily for 800m to Hey Moss, where at SE 07850 01140 another path crosses the route from NNW to SSE. Ignore it and continue on your original path as it veers temporarily SW for 100m to SE 07800 01100. There, it proceeds south again, then SSW, dropping steadily downwards and joining a track at SE 07500 00330.

The route continues south for 500m, rounding an old quarry, one that contributed much of the stone that built the railway along the valley and constructed the reservoir dams. As it curves around the SW side of the quarry, leave the track and take the stile at SK 07300 99770, following the path south down a very steep descent. It's precarious walking, hard on the feet, the path littered with rocks that can be slippery, loose, or both. Arriving at the bottom, take the stile immediately in front, then follow the track around to the right (west). Cross the ladder stile on to another drive and walk 300m south down to the junction adjacent to the Crowden campsite. Finally, follow the walled track to the facility block and turn left through the wooded area back to the car park.

Route summary

Your present location	Your next objective	Waypoint at next objective	Directions
Start, Crowden SK 07250 99270	Pennine Way signpost, indicating left	SK 07170 99420	West from car park and right up to T-Junction
SK 07170 99420	Second Pennine Way signpost, indicating right	SK 06870 99070	400m, over the brook and dyke
SK 06870 99070	Gate, with path to Lad's Leap leaving to the west	SK 06720 99470	400m, keep straight on after the gate
SK 06720 99470	Clough	SE 06290 00400	1.1km NNW, passing below Black Tor
SE 06290 00400	Oaken Clough	SE 05850 00940	750m NW, take the left fork after the clough
SE 05850 00940	Top of Ladlow Rocks, path forks	SE 05670 01300	450m from clough, take the left path at the fork
SE 05670 01300	Boundary fence and stile	SE 05390 01630	400m NW along gully track
SE 05390 01630	Featherbed Moss pillar	SE 04643 01169	900m across the moor on a 240 deg bearing
SE 04643 01169	Boundary fence and stile	SE 05390 01630	Retrace your steps, 900m NE (60 deg)
SE 05390 01630	Top of Ladlow Rocks	SE 05670 01300	Retrace the route, then turn NNE along the top
SE 05670 01300	Point where path drops to level of the clough	SE 06100 02600	1.5km NNE, marshy areas ahead
SE 06100 02600	Stile in second boundary fence	SE 07130 04190	2km, N and then NE, a paved path helps
SE 07130 04190	Holme Moss pillar	SE 07816 04684	900m NW from the stile
SE 07816 04684	Fence stile	SE 07990 04370	400m SSE (138 deg) across pathless moor
SE 07990 04370	Cairn	SE 08070 04200	200m SSE, peat path and groughs ahead
SE 08070 04200	Point where path veers from SE to SSE	SE 08370 03850	500m SE, terrain changes to grass moor
SE 08370 03850	Marker post on Tooleyshaw Moor	SE 08540 02990	900m SSE (174 deg) along grass moor path
SE 08540 02990	White Low	SE 08440 02250	400m SSE, then turning for 400m SSW
SE 08440 02250	Marker post on Westend Moss	SE 08200 01890	A further 400m SSW
SE 08200 01890	Hey Moss, where another path crosses	SE 07850 01140	800m SSW. Now the route deviates SW
SE 07850 01140	Point where path turns back south	SE 07800 01100	Just 100m, but a tricky spot on the route
SE 07800 01100	Where path joins a track	SE 07500 00330	900m SSW
SE 07500 00330	Stile for final descent	SK 07300 99770	500m SSW, after quarry
SK 07300 99770	Crowden, back to start	SK 07250 99270	Steep descent, then a driveway to campsite

Walk 2 – Dead Edge End, Snailsden and South Nab

Start: Roadside pull-off on the Windle Edge minor road off the A628, 700m NE of Salter's Brook Bridge – Map Reference SE 14100 00680

Distance: 15.1km (9.5 miles)

Total ascent: 360m (1170 ft)

Estimated time: 5 hours

Grading: Moderate, but difficult in low cloud or with lying snow

OS map: Explorer map OL 1 The Peak District – Dark Peak area

The route

From the start, the route crosses the moor to the Dead Edge End pillar, then follows a county boundary fence before crossing Grains Moss to the Snailsden pillar. From there the walk takes in the Winscar reservoir, before crossing Gallows Moss around the Windleden reservoir and visiting the South Nab pillar. The final leg is along a moor path running parallel to the main road, passing the ancient Lady Cross route marker.

The height profile shows a gentle incline up to the Dead Edge End pillar, relatively level walking across the moor to Snailsden, but with a stiffer climb from Windleden reservoir to the South Nab summit.

The walk

Enter the Open Access moorland via a stile gate on the west side of the lane, following the worn grass track west, then NW, for 700m, reaching a small brick building at SE 13540 01100. Close by to the SW is another such structure, one of several air shafts built to ventilate the three-mile long Woodhead rail tunnel that runs from Dunford Bridge to near Woodhead itself.

Completed in 1845, it was the first railway between Sheffield and Manchester, claiming the lives of 32 men during its construction, with another 140 seriously injured. When it was extended to include a second tunnel in 1852, another 26 men perished. In fact, it was alleged that, statistically, it was safer to be at the battle of Waterloo than to be a labourer constructing the Woodhead tunnel!

After years of steam, with appalling conditions for any man working in the tunnel, including signalmen on long shifts, a new tunnel was built alongside the others. It was completed in 1954, that one being electrified, and costing only six lives. So Health and Safety legislation had at last made its mark! The tunnel was last used 1981.

Leaving the brick buildings at SE 13540 01100, turn NNE for 250m, initially

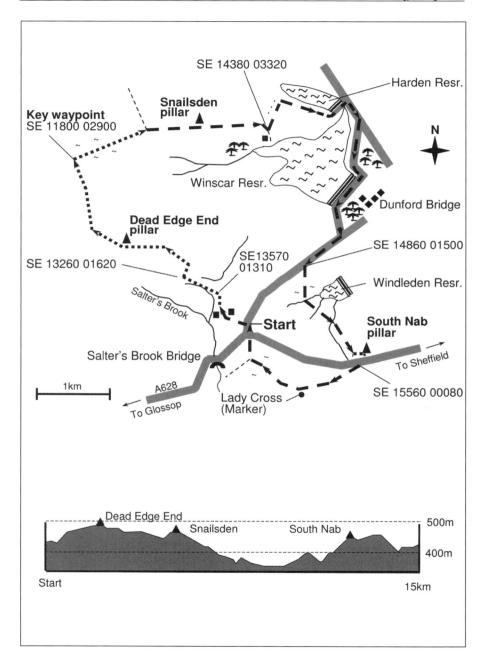

SE 14380 03320

Harden Resr.

Snailsden pillar

Key waypoint
SE 11800 02900

N

Winscar Resr.

Dunford Bridge

Dead Edge End pillar

SE 14860 01500

SE 13260 01620

SE13570 01310

Windleden Resr.

Salter's Brook

Start

South Nab pillar

Salter's Brook Bridge

To Sheffield

1km

A628

SE 15560 00080

To Glossop

Lady Cross (Marker)

Dead Edge End

500m

Snailsden

South Nab

400m

Start

15km

following the remains of a vehicle track, and then using a narrow grass path to reach the boundary edge of the moorland peat at around SE 13570 01310. Follow the peat line generally NW, always keeping to the NE shoulder of the clough and following a lightly used path, the route eventually reaching the county boundary fence at SE 13260 01620. From there it is only 100m NE to the point where the fence turns sharply to the west. After that it's easy to follow its northern side for the next 1km, up to the Dead Edge End pillar. The walking is not difficult, a faint path through the short moorland grass having been established alongside the fence, but at one spot there is a tricky bridge to cross over a particularly wide ditch.

The pillar is in good condition, positioned against the west side of the fence, with its spider and flush bracket intact, and a stone plug replacing the lost OS insert. In the picture, the fence continues relentlessly into the distance, marking the route to be followed northwards from the trig point.

The pillar details are:

Position: SE 12445 01728
Flush bracket No: S1779
Height: 500m (1625 ft)
Horizon: 80km (50 miles)
Built: May 1937
Historic use: Secondary
Current use: None
Condition: Good

Dead Edge End pillar

Visibility from Dead Edge End to other nearby pillars is relatively poor, with only Margery Hill, Outer Edge and the other two pillars on this walk (Snailsden and South Nab) being in clear view. The pillars to the eastern half of the compass are generally low-lying (some just about in view), and the extensive moors around the south, west and NW restrict line-of-sight in those directions.

From the pillar, continue along the east side of the fence for 1.5km, walking first WNW, then NNW, to a key waypoint at SE 11800 02900. There, turn east to face ENE, ready to cross the moor towards the Snailsden pillar. 150m before reaching that point, the county boundary

Pillar	Distance	Direction
Snailsden	1.8km	NNE (025 deg)
Pool Hill *	14.2km	NENE (060 deg)
Hill Top Farm *	15.3km	EESE (099 deg)
Whitwell Moor *	13.3km	ESE (110 deg)
Outer Edge	7.1km	SE (132 deg)
Margery Hill (Primary)	8.8km	SE (133 deg)
Featherbed Moss *	7.8km	W (265 deg)
Holme Moss (Primary) *	5.5km	NWNW (303 deg)
West Nab	8.5km	WNNW (326 deg)
South Nab	3.5km	ESE (114 deg)

* The visibility to these pillars is marginal

divides. But only the NW-leading boundary continues as a fence, the one leading NE being marked by a sequence of low posts, some of which you'll encounter later when crossing the moor towards Snailsden.

Before starting for Snailsden, set your GPS objective as SE 12750 03340, which is 1km distant on a 066 deg bearing. It's not directly towards the pillar, but the route avoids the deepest groughs. The terrain is a difficult mixture of moorland grass and heather, but can be negotiated with a little forward planning, often making use of the areas that have been recently burned as part of the land management. Having reached the objective, turn due east and reset your GPS for SE 13198 03311 (Snailsden pillar). Walk diagonally up the incline for 450m to the trig point, making use of any paths that you find. The precise compass bearing is 092 deg.

Snailsden pillar is in poor condition, with the top badly eroded and the spider (with its plastic plug) in danger of becoming detached. But it's perhaps interesting to see how well the bronze alloy resists corrosion, whilst the concrete around it has succumbed to the weather.

The pillar details are:

Position: SE 13198 03311
Flush bracket No: S1780
Height: 476m (1547 ft)
Horizon: 78km (49 miles)
Built: May 1937
Historic use: Secondary
Current use: None
Condition: Poor

Snailsden pillar

As from Dead Edge End, visibility to other pillars from Snailsden is relatively poor, but a few more of the low-lying sites to the north round to SE just about come into view.

Leaving the Snailsden pillar, follow the well-worn vehicle track eastwards across the moor. The walking is relatively easy, and the views to the fore expand to reveal the Winscar reservoir, with its distinctive blue/green-coloured dam. After 1km, the path turns SE for 200m and joins a track crossing the route at SE 14380 03320. Turn left there (NNE), walking 400m through a line of grouse butts, before turning right (ESE) and following the track for 800m to the Harden reservoir dam. Cross it, following the narrow access drive that emerges on to a lane on the other side.

From there, the route follows the lane south for 400m into the entrance for the Winscar reservoir parking and viewing area. Passing along the eastern edge of the water and then SE across the dam, you may be lucky enough to witness yachts in competition, the sailors pitting their skills against the fickle wind conditions generated by the complex shape of the reservoir. From the SE side of the

Pillar	Distance	Direction
Haw Cliff Top *	7.4km	NNE (026 deg)
The Heights	14.8km	ENNE (033 deg)
Pool Hill *	12.8km	ENE (065 deg)
Hill Top Farm	14.9km	EESE (106 deg)
Whitwell Moor *	13.2km	ESE (117 deg)
South Nab	3.9km	ESSE (141 deg)
Outer Edge	7.8km	ESSE (144 deg)
Dead Edge End	1.8km	SSW (206 deg)
Holme Moss (Primary) *	5.5km	WSW (248 deg)
West Nab	7.8km	NW (314 deg)
Crossland Heath	11.0km	NNNW (346 deg)
Wolfstones Height	5.8km	NNNW (352 deg)

* The visibility to these pillars is marginal

dam parapet there is an excellent view of Dunford Bridge, a place where the residents must occasionally look up at the dam and wonder about its integrity! Also visible from the parapet are the long disused Woodhead tunnel exits and the old railway cuttings, emerging from the tree-lined hillside to the south.

From the SE end of the dam, go south, regaining the lane, then turning SW and walking 600m to a footpath sign on the left that also warns of wet conditions (SE 14860 01500). It marks the route across the head of the Windleden reservoirs and, although it can be very wet after heavy rain, it is not too difficult. The path is part of the 'Barnsley Boundary Walk', taking the route south from the stile at the lane down through moorland grass and reeds to the first of three cloughs that feed the reservoir, each with bridging boards at the crossing points.

After the first, the path bears left (SE) at a wrought-iron fence and leads on to the second stream. On the other side, the ground rises steeply, the path reaching a stile at SE 15090 00820 before continuing to the third clough. Cross it and follow the path on the east side of the stream for the next 600m, generally south, to a point at SE 15440 00280. From there, turn off the path, walking eastwards (bearing 081 deg) across the moor for 200m to reach the final pillar, South Nab.

The pillar is in good condition, the spider is secure, but there is a plastic plug replacing the lost

Dunford, from the Winscar dam

OS insert. The picture shows the view to the NNW, across the Windleden reservoirs. Although not on any official route, the faint paths through the grass show that the pillar is often visited.

The pillar details are:

Position: SE 15629 00319
Flush bracket No: S1770
Height: 461m (1498 ft)
Horizon: 77km (48 miles)
Built: May 1937
Historic use: Secondary
Current use: None
Condition: Good

South Nab pillar

Pillar	Distance	Direction
Hoyland Swaine	10.9km	ENE (066 deg)
Hill Top Farm	12.0km	E (095 deg)
Whitwell Moor *	9.8km	ESE (108 deg)
Outer Edge	3.9km	ESSE (148 deg)
Wild Bank	16.9km	WWSW (262 deg)
Featherbed Moss	10.9km	W (274 deg)
Dead Edge End	3.5km	WNW (294 deg)
Holme Moss (Primary) *	8.9km	NWNW (299 deg)
West Nab	11.6km	NW (316 deg)
Snailsden	3.9km	WNNW (321 deg)

* The visibility to these pillars is marginal

There is line-of-sight to ten local pillars from South Nab, mainly in the SE and NW quadrants. Views to pillars in the south and SW are blocked by the extensive moors. But to the west, Wild Bank is in sight (in square SJ, near Stalybridge), a pillar that is not visible from either Dead Edge End or Snailsden. To the south, the Primary at Margery Hill is close by, but blocked by Outer Edge on the same bearing.

From the pillar, walk south, following the west side of a stone wall, emerging through a stile gate on to the A628 roadside verge. Follow the road west for 150m, crossing to a stile gate on the south side, at SE 15560 00080. It leads to a wide grass track that runs WSW across the moor, passing a small memorial at SK 15360 99980 and reaching the ancient Lady Cross marker post at SK 14850 99750, after 800m. The history of the marker is unknown, but it's positioned on a high point, with paths leaving in three directions.

From the cross, the grass moor path

Lady Cross marker post

veers NW for 800m, emerging via a stile on to a limestone track (Trans Pennine Trail) at SE 14080 00110. The last 200m, prior to the stile, is across some very wet ground, but it's possible to walk along the remains of a stone wall to avoid the worst. From the other side of the stile, follow the track north for 400m, emerging again at the main road, with the lane and parking area to the fore.

Route summary

Your present location	Your next objective	Waypoint at next objective	Directions
Roadside pull-off SE 14100 00680	Brick building	SE 13540 01100	700m west and NW along grass track
SE 13540 01100	Boundary of moorland peat	SE 13570 01310	250m NNE along old vehicle track
SE 13570 01310	County boundary fence (CBF)	SE 13260 01620	400m NW along north edge of clough
SE 13260 01620	Dead Edge End pillar	SE 12445 01728	First, 100m NE to CBF corner, then 1km west along CBF
SE 12445 01728	Point from where to turn NE, ready to cross the moor – **Key waypoint**	SE 11800 02900	1.5km generally NW. The location is 150m NW of the point where the CBF turns WNW
SE 11800 02900	Point on moor below north end of Snailsden ridge	SE 12750 03340	1km ENE (bearing 066 deg) across the moor
SE 12750 03340	Snailsden pillar	SE 13198 03311	450m east (bearing 092 deg), diagonally up the incline
SE 13198 03311	Track crossing the route	SE 14380 03320	1.7km east along vehicle track, go left
SE 14380 03320	Lane by Harden reservoir	SE 15380 03700	400m NNE on track, then 1.1km west around the reservoir
SE 15380 03700	Winscar reservoir dam	SE 15560 02680	1km south on lane and past reservoir car park
SE 15560 02680	Sign post for wet footpath leaving the lane	SE 14860 01500	1.5km, total, over dam, left to lane, SW down lane
SE 14860 01500	Gallows Clough	SE 14820 00970	500m south on wet path
SE 14820 00970	Stile	SE 15090 00820	350m SE, over second clough
SE 15090 00820	Point to leave path towards pillar	SE 15440 00280	650m SSE along path, over third clough
SE 15440 00280	South Nab pillar	SE 15629 00319	200m east across moor (bearing 081 deg)
SE 15629 00319	Stile gate on south side of main road	SE 15560 00080	300m total, south to road, then west
SE 15560 00080	Lady Cross marker post	SK 14850 99750	800m SW on wide grass track
SK 14850 99750	Stile to limestone track (Trans Pennine Way)	SE 14080 00110	900m NW along track, very wet area at end
SE 14080 00110	Back to start at road side pull-off	SE 14100 00680	600m north on track and across the main road

Walk 3 – Higher Shelf Stones and Cock Hill

Start: High point on the A57 Snake Pass between Glossop and Sheffield – Map reference SK 08800 92910

Distance: 17km (10.6 miles)

Total ascent: 540m (1750 ft)

Estimated time: 6 hours

Grading: Difficult; do not attempt when deep snow is lying

OS map: Explorer map OL 1 The Peak District – Dark Peak area

The route

The route follows the Pennine Way NE from the A57 trunk road, with a detour across the moor to visit the Higher Shelf Stones pillar and an aircraft crash site, before turning north to Bleaklow Head. The next leg is on established paths, with a short diversion to visit the Cock Hill pillar, followed by a descent to the outskirts of Old Glossop and then the final long haul up the Doctor's Gate path to complete the walk.

The height profile shows the long ascent at the end of the walk. Note that the Cock Hill pillar is not on an obvious peak, with Glossop Low (slightly to the left of the trig on the profile) being higher.

The walk

From the road, proceed NNE towards Bleaklow moor and to the first landmark, the 'Old Woman' crossing, where the Doctor's Gate path intersects the Pennine Way. The origin of the name 'Old Woman' is not understood, but according to local legend, the 'Doctor' was a Longdendale man who challenged the Devil to a horse race and, much to the irritation of the Devil, won!

In fact, the Devil is a recurring theme on this walk, with the 'Devil's Dyke' being the next part of the route, walking due NE along the Pennine Way. It is here that mysterious lights are sometimes seen, claimed to be the burning torches of Roman soldiers as they return to haunt the path they used nearly 2000 years ago. They are just

Marker post

some of the ethereal lights said to be regularly seen on Bleaklow. Following the path, look out for the small marker stones. They are a great help in poor weather or when there is snow on the ground.

To reach the Higher Shelf Stones pillar and the aircraft crash site requires a detour from the path across an area of open peat moor. The need to proceed with care, especially in very wet conditions, is all too obvious. To reach the crash site, leave the main path from the marker post situated at SK 09720 94800 and head west across the moor. The marker is at the spot where the Pennine Way joins Hern Clough, which flows away to the east.

In thick cloud, a GPS or compass is essential, setting the waypoint objective as SK 09060 94880, which is the crash site. The exact compass bearing from the

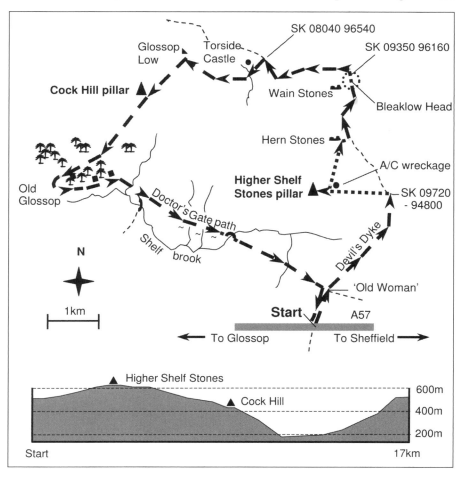

Aircraft crash site

marker post is 275 deg (nearly due west). The site is only 700m from the Pennine Way, but it can seem a long way when the weather is poor. There are some vague paths, but most of the route is across peat hags and around the groughs, and with a compass only it may be helpful to use the 'walk to' method described in the Introduction section.

The crash site itself is extensive, with a great deal of debris to examine. It was a USAF Superfortress RB-29A called 'Overexposed' that crashed in 1948 on its way from Scampton to the Burtonwood airbase, possibly delivering the payroll. A memorial at the site describes how all thirteen crew on board perished in the crash. It is believed that the name of the aircraft derived from its role of photo-reconnaissance during the early atom bomb tests. Note that the site belongs to the Ministry of Defence, and the removal of any part of the aircraft is prohibited. 'Take nothing but photographs, and leave nothing but footprints' is an appropriate maxim.

From the aircraft crash site, take a SW heading, the pillar quickly coming into view some 200m distant across the moor. It looks out over the Doctor's Gate path (the old Roman road) and the A57 Snake Pass, with vistas extending to Kinder Scout in the south, Glossop to the west and Saddleworth Moor to the NW. The easterly views all look across the daunting Bleaklow Moor.

The pillar is a concrete structure, in reasonably good condition, painted white on two sides and with the flush bracket and spider both intact. There is a stone plug in the spider, replacing the lost OS insert. Historically, it was one of the Secondary pillars, but has no current use.

The Shelf Stones themselves, including the rocks adjacent to the pillar, bear witness to the names and dates of others having passed this way over many years, even before the trig point was erected.

The pillar details are:

Position: SK 08894 94787
Flush bracket No: S2627
Height: 621m (2020 ft)
Horizon: 89km (56 miles)
Built: June 1939
Historic use: Secondary
Current use: None
Condition: Good

Higher Shelf Stones pillar

The pillar triangulates through line-of-sight with at least 11 others, including three Primary pillars. On a very clear day, and with binoculars or telescope, it should be possible to pick out the closest. Cock Hill, the second pillar on this walk, is not quite visible, being obscured by the high ground to the NW.

Pillar	Distance	Direction
Outer Edge (Howden)	9.1km	EENE (076 deg)
Margery Hill (Primary)	10.0km	E (085 deg)
Back Tor	11.5km	ESE (109 deg)
West End Moor	4.3km	ESE (111 deg)
Edale Moor	8.1km	SSE (150 deg)
The Edge (Kinder, Primary)	5.6km	SSSW (193 deg)
Harry Hut	6.0km	SW (228 deg)
Cown Edge Rocks *	7.3km	WSW (248 deg)
Wild Bank	10.5km	WNW (288 deg)
Featherbed Moss	7.7km	WNNW (327 deg)
Holme Moss (Primary)	10.0km	N (354 deg)

* Pillar destroyed

Having bagged the pillar, the next step is to regain the Pennine Way. The route first returns NE to the crash site, then heads NNE to the distinctive Hern Stones (SK 09220 95340). The best starting point when back at the crash site is the small memorial, leaving it northwards, and then turning NNE with the faint path. The distance and bearing from the crash site to Hern Stones is 400m, 018 deg. From Hern Stones it is 200m due east to regain the Pennine Way. (Aim for SK 09420 95390). The terrain between the crash site and Hern Stones, and then on to the main Pennine Way is difficult, with more peat hags and groughs to negotiate. Often, it is better to follow the bottom of a grough as it winds and wanders, but there are no hard and fast rules.

Once back on the Pennine Way, follow it north to the high point (633m) at Bleaklow Head. There are more path markers to point the way, and Bleaklow Head itself is identified by a distinctive cairn (SK 09340 96000). For those who want to visit the three 'Wayne Stones', precariously perched on their rock plinth, they are 200m SW of the cairn, at SK 09190 95910. But it's then important to return to the cairn before continuing the walk.

Locating the correct way onwards from Bleaklow Head can be tricky, as many 'apparent' paths leave the area, only to fade out. It is important to locate the route that runs NNW (again the Pennine Way) from a point near SK 09350 96160. Straying too far to the NE instead of north quickly leads to some very difficult terrain. The best policy is to stand by the cairn; then the path should be clearly visible, running NNW.

Following that path across Far Moss, after 400m the route reaches a fence at SK 09210 96580. Turn west there and follow the stream for 1.1km, eventually reaching the junction with Torside Clough. Cross to its west bank and follow it north for 120m, looking for a track that branches westwards (at SK 08040 96540) past Torside Castle. It can be easy to miss, particularly in poor weather, so pace the distance carefully.

The so-called 'Castle' is no more than a round hill, which may be a Bronze Age burial ground, or just as easily a local mound of clay left by the retreating glaciers. Whatever it is, the people of Glossop regularly report mysterious lights and flares hovering over the landscape, and in keeping with the Bleaklow tradition, they call them the 'Devil's Bonfires'. The explanations are myriad, including spirits, aliens, escaping burning methane and electrostatic build-up over geological faults.

From that point, the route continues due west, the path often being obscure. Avoid taking a direct line towards the Cock Hill pillar; turn NW instead across the source of Small Clough at around SK 06950 96420, then walk 400m up to Glossop Low. At the top there is a partially built stone hut, a useful place to take some refreshment before starting the final leg.

From Glossop Low, take the path SW past a line of grouse butts and head for a point on the path that is 100m due SE of the Cock Hill pillar (at SK 06020 96090). There, look for the small path that heads across to the trig point. The pillar is positioned below the more obvious peak of Glossop Low, so that it looks out over the town of Glossop. It is concrete, well preserved, recently painted and with a plastic plug in the spider replacing the original Ordnance Survey insert.

The pillar details are:

Position: SK 05931 96189
Flush bracket No: S2780
Height: 427m (1388 ft)
Horizon: 74km (46 miles)
Built: April 1940
Historic use: Secondary
Current use: None
Condition: Good

The pillar triangulates with only five others, all to the south and west. Views east are blocked by Bleaklow,

Cock Hill pillar

Pillar	Distance	Direction
The Edge (Kinder, Primary) **	7.1km	SSSE (165 deg)
Harry Hut	5.6km	SSSW (195 deg)
Cown Edge Rocks *	5.6km	SW (222 deg)
Werneth Low	11.1km	WSW (249 deg)
Wild Bank	7.3km	WWNW (284 deg)

* Pillar destroyed ** Visibility to The Edge is marginal

and those to the north by Peaknaze Moor. Lantern Pike, where the pillar is toppled, is only just out of sight to the SSW. The pillar at Higher Shelf Stones is not in sight.

From Cock Hill (which might have been a popular meeting place for cock-fighting, but that is by no means certain), the path heads SW and then WSW as it follows a track flanked by two stone walls. It is not clearly marked as such on many maps, but provides an easy route down into the outskirts of Old Glossop.

After the stile at the bottom, turn left along Charles Street, then south into Hope Street and follow it round to the next junction. Turn left there, this track becoming the Doctor's Gate path that will lead the way home. The first section is easy walking, just keep to the path and avoid any tracks that lead to the east; they lead back up to either 'Shelf Benches' or 'James Thorn'.

The middle section of the Doctor's Gate path can be very boggy, even after a long dry spell, so pick the route with care, particularly on the steep areas where water is oozing across the path. Finally, the last section is rocky and steep, a little hard on the feet, but with splendid views back down the track. At the top, the path again reaches the 'Old Woman', a welcome sight, with the road and car not far away to the west.

Route summary

Your present location	Your next objective	Waypoint at next objective	Directions
Start, Snake Pass SK 08800 92910	'Old Woman' Crossing (The point of return)	SK 08990 93320	500m NNE on Pennine Way
SK 08990 93320	A point 1.2km NE along 'Devil's Dyke' path	SK 09840 94210	A clear path with marker posts, 1.2km NE
SK 09840 94210	Hern Clough marker post	SK 09720 94800	600m N and NW. Then leave the path to the west at the post
SK 09720 94800	Aircraft crash site, across the moor, few paths	SK 09060 94880	700m west, bearing 275 deg
SK 09060 94880	HSS pillar. (Visible from the crash site)	SK 08894 94787	200m SW from crash site
SK 08894 94787	Back to crash site	SK 09060 94880	Retrace your steps, 200m NE
SK 09060 94880	Hern Stones, across the moor, no paths	SK 09220 95340	500m NNE from crash site, bearing 018 deg
SK 09220 95340	Regain the Pennine Way path	SK 09420 95390	200m east across the moor, no clear paths
SK 09420 95390	Bleaklow Head	SK 09340 96000	800m generally north along Pennine Way
SK 09340 96000	Exit from Bleaklow Head (BH)	SK 09350 96160	It's important to find the correct path to the north
SK 09350 96160	A fence by a clough (Wildboar Grain)	SK 09210 96580	450m NNW from BH, across Far Moss
SK 09210 96580	Join Torside Clough, then cross to its west side	SK 08080 96440	1.2km W along Wildboar Grain
SK 08080 96440	A path branching west, easy to miss	SK 08040 96540	Only 120m NNW along Torside Clough
SK 08040 96540	Top of Small Clough	SK 06950 96420	1.2km West, past Torside Castle
SK 06950 96420	Summit of Glossop Low. Look for old stone hut	SK 06630 96730	450m NW from Small Clough
SK 06630 96730	Path that goes NW to Cock Hill pillar	SK 06020 96090	800m SW from Glossop Low, down a line of grouse butts
SK 06020 96090	Cock Hill pillar	SK 05931 96189	100m NW on indistinct path
SK 05931 96189	Stile at Old Glossop, into Charles Street	SK 04460 94970	2km from pillar, first SW, then WSW
SK 04460 94970	Start of Doctor's Gate path	SK 04570 94830	250m east, then south down Hope Street
SK 04570 94830	'Old Woman' crossing	SK 09900 93320	Follow the Doctor's Gate path E and SE for 5km
SK 09900 93320	Back to start	SK 08800 92910	500m SSW, familiar ground

Walk 4 – Margery Hill and Outer Edge

Start: At the King's Oak terminus, northern end of the Howden reservoir road – Map Reference SK 16730 94050

Distance: 10km (6.0 miles)

Total ascent: 370m (1200 ft)

Estimated time: 3.5 hours

Grading: Moderate

OS map: Explorer map OL 1 The Peak District – Dark Peak area

The route

The route begins at King's Oak, follows the River Derwent northwards to the Slippery Stones bridge, turns east along Cranberry Clough and rises to the Margery Hill summit. From there it returns NW along Howden Edge to the Outer Edge pillar, with two small excursions to view aircraft crash sites. From Outer Edge, the route continues over Crow Stones Edge, past a third aircraft crash site, down Broadhead Clough and on to the lower path south for the return.

Note on parking and bus services

During weekdays and Saturdays, limited parking is possible along the reservoir road and near to the King's Oak terminus (the limit of travel for vehicles). On Sundays and Bank Holidays, parking is restricted to specific areas between the A57 and the Fairholmes Visitor Centre, as well as at the Centre itself, with no tourist traffic allowed along the road to King's Oak.

A regular bus service runs from the Fairholmes facility to King's Oak, the earliest departure being at 09.35am and the last pick-up from King's Oak back to Fairholmes being at 16.30pm. For further details of full and current timetable, ring 'Stagecoach' on 0870 608 2608.

The height profile shows a symmetrical walk, a steady ascent, level walking on top, then a steady descent.

The walk

From King's Oak, follow the limestone track that skirts the upper reaches of the Howden reservoir, ultimately following the course of the River Derwent to the 'Slippery Stones' bridge at SK 16960 95120.

First constructed in the seventeenth century, the old stone packhorse bridge originally stood in the village of Derwent, around 300m south of where the Derwent dam is now situated. Before the valley was flooded, the stones were recovered and stored, and it was in 1959, encouraged by public subscription, that the

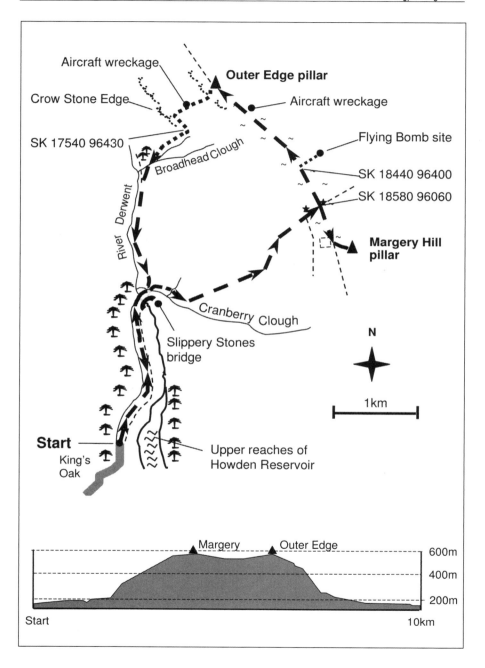

Aircraft wreckage

Crow Stone Edge

SK 17540 96430

Broadhead Clough

River Derwent

Outer Edge pillar

Aircraft wreckage

Flying Bomb site

SK 18440 96400

SK 18580 96060

Margery Hill pillar

Cranberry Clough

Slippery Stones bridge

N

1km

Start

King's Oak

Upper reaches of Howden Reservoir

Margery   Outer Edge

600m

400m

200m

Start

10km

Looking back down Cranberry Clough

old bridge was re-erected at its current site. A memorial stone, inset into the wall on the western approach, states that the bridge stands as a tribute to John Derry, who inspired others with his love of the Derbyshire and Yorkshire hills.

Passing over the bridge, the route takes a NNE heading towards the mouth of Cranberry Clough, where it crosses the stream over a boarded bridge before reaching a fork at SK 17040 95360. Take the path to the right (east), identified on the marker post as a bridle path. (The path to the left, marked 'Walkers only', is the return route). The route then follows Cranberry Clough for 400m before crossing Bull Clough and rising steeply up a well-worn path, marked in places by rough stone steps. At the top, the path reverts to sandstone, coming to a fork at SK 17520 95260. Turn left there (NE), walking uphill away from the clough and around the north of the hillside. It's well worth a look back from this point, with excellent views down to the mouth of the clough and, in the distance, the Slippery Stones bridge.

As the gradient slackens, the path crosses a well-worn grassy area, winding its way across the open moor. A paved section, starting at SK 18100 95630, then provides easy walking up to a point 300m from the top of Howden Edge. Near the top, the route reaches the first of two cairns. It is the second of these, at SK 18580 96060, that marks the route that runs along the Edge. Turn right there (SSE), following a very wide, usually wet path across the peat up to a fenced area of moor that has been set aside for conservation. Passing that area to the left (east), follow the fence to the SE corner and then turn ESE towards Margery Hill pillar. The path is usually boggy, threading a route between the groughs, but better than nothing.

Margery pillar is a Primary (as denoted by the flush bracket number, with no preceding 'S'), with reasonable all-round views. It's set on a solid stone base, so that the site has not suffered the same level of erosion that is common around the peat moor pillars. The original plug has been lost, replaced by a plastic insert, but the overall condition is fair.

Margery Hill pillar

The pillar details are:

Position: SK 18911 95695
Flush bracket No: 2965
Height: 546m (1775 ft)
Horizon: 84km (52 miles)
Built: Summer 1936
Historic use: Primary
Current use: None
Condition: Fair

Pillar	Distance	Direction
Pool Hill	14.3km	NNE (024 deg)
Hoyland Swaine	11.3km	ENNE (036 deg)
Whitwell Moor	6.2km	EENE (076 deg)
Kirk Edge *	9.2km	ESE (107 deg)
Ox Stones	15.5km	ESSE (144 deg)
Stanage Edge	14.1km	SSE (154 deg)
Winhill Pike *	10.6km	S (181 deg)
Bradwell Moor	16.6km	SSW (200 deg)
Mam Tor	13.5km	SSW (207 deg)
Edale Moor *	9.9km	WSSW (217 deg)
The Edge (Primary)	12.9km	SWSW (240 deg)
West End Moor	6.5km	WSW (248 deg)
Higher Shelf Stones	10.1km	W (265 deg)
Featherbed Moss	15.2km	WNW (291 deg)
Holme Moss (Primary)	14.2km	NWNW (309 deg)
Dead Edge End	8.8km	NW (313 deg)
Outer Edge	1.7km	NW (317 deg)

* The visibility to these pillars is marginal

From Margery Hill, there is line-of-sight to 17 local pillars, including the two Primaries at Holme Moss and The Edge. Back Tor, which is close by to the south, is obscured by Howden Moor. The visibility to Kirk Edge is marginal, and Emlin Ridge, which is closer and on a similar bearing, is just hidden by Hobson Moss.

Taking a more distant perspective reveals that it has views to three other Primaries, including Harland South, which is near Matlock in the south of the Peak District.

From the pillar, retrace the route back to the cairn at SK18580 96060, continuing NNW along the Howden Edge path. Again, it's usually very wet. At SK18440 96400, leave the edge path in a NE direction, following another path that is no more than a narrow rut, making your GPS objective as SK18570 96520, which is the site of a V1 Flying Bomb explosion. The walking is surprisingly easy, and after 180m, the path leads to a blackened peat scar, providing a stark contrast with the surrounding grass moor. With just a compass, and in poor visibility, finding the narrow path will not be easy. From the cairn, it is 375m on a 333 deg bearing along the Edge path, and should take no more than 15 minutes at normal walking pace.

It was on the 24th December 1944 that a Heinkel 111 German bomber air-launched a V1 Flying Bomb off the east coast of England, setting it towards its target, the city of Manchester. Fortunately, it landed (without exploding) some 25km short of its objective at this bleak moorland spot. For safety, it was blown up where it lay by a bomb-disposal team, and the circular peat scar has remained to this day, unclaimed by the grass and heather. For some years, fragments of the casing were evident in and around the crater, but many of those have since been removed by souvenir hunters. Occasionally, a new fragment will surface from the peat, but at the authors' last visit, none was visible.

From the site, retrace your steps to the Howden Edge path at SK18440 96400, then continue walking NW towards the Outer Edge pillar, 1km distant, at SK 17703 96973. As usual, numerous detours are required to manoeuvre round the groughs. Half way to the pillar, at SK 18040 96740, and within 20m of the path, are the small remains of an Airspeed Oxford aircraft that crashed on 18th October 1943 during a navigational exercise. There is just a small amount of wreckage, tucked away in a grough, with a single wooden cross to commemorate the dead crew.

Continuing NW along the main path again, it is 400m to the Outer Edge pillar. The site is badly eroded, with the base completely exposed, another testimony to the popularity of these landmarks with walkers. Other than that, the pillar is intact, with a plastic insert replacing the original OS plug. The pillar also carries a small plate commemorating the life of a dog named Penny, "Who loved to run in these hills". She died on 14th March 1998, aged 15 years. It is not the first pillar that dedicated walkers have used to remember a fellow rambler, human or canine.

The pillar details are:

Position: SK 17703 96973
Flush bracket No: S1771
Height: 542m (1761 ft)
Horizon: 83km (52 miles)
Built: May 1937
Historic use: Secondary
Current use: None
Condition: Fair

From the Outer Edge pillar there is line-of-sight to 15 local pillars, most of them the same as those visible from Margery. But Mam Tor is just out of sight and Featherbed Moss is obscured by the area of moor called Horse Stone.

The Outer Edge pillar

Pillar	Distance	Direction
Pool Hill	13.7km	ENNE (031 deg)
Hoyland Swaine *	11.4km	NE (045 deg)
Hill Top Farm	10.1km	EENE (077 deg)
Kirk Edge	10.7km	ESE (112 deg)
Margery Hill (Primary)	1.7km	SE (137 deg)
Winhill Pike *	11.9km	S (175 deg)
Bradwell Moor	17.4km	SSSW (195 deg)
Edale Moor	10.3km	SSW (207 deg)
West End Moor	6.1km	SWSW (232 deg)
The Edge (Primary)	12.6km	SWSW (232 deg)
Higher Shelf Stones	9.1km	WWSW (256 deg)
Holme Moss (Primary)	12.5km	NWNW (308 deg)
Dead Edge End	7.1km	NW (312 deg)
Snailsden	7.8km	WNNW (324 deg)
South Nab	3.9km	WNNW (328 deg)

* The visibility to these pillars is marginal

From the pillar, take a due south heading along a small path that leads to the Outer Edge Rocks at SK 17710 96880. Navigating your way through the rocks, turn SW and use the small path that descends for 400m across the moor towards Crowstones Edge. The path follows a line of grouse butts to a point at SK 17410 96610, where there is more aircraft wreckage. It originates from an Airspeed Consul that crashed on 12th April 1951. Although it's not on a regular walking route, this is another site that has fallen prey to the souvenir hunters, with much of the smaller material having been removed. Thankfully, the traditional small wooden crosses that provide a memorial to the crew who perished have remained undisturbed.

From the crash site, continue SW for 100m to Crowstones Edge, using the continuation of the path that located the wreckage, and passing more grouse butts on the way. At the Edge, turn SE for 250m, passing beyond the end of the outcrop and aiming for SK 17540 96430, which is a position immediately above Broadhead Clough. From this area, the views to the valley in front are excellent, the route down winding its way around the hillside.

At SK 17540 96430 turn SW and, using one of the many lightly trodden paths, begin your descent. These paths were probably used to access the grouse butts, and eventually they converge into one, that path then following the clough down and crossing over a stream at the bottom (SK 17120 96180). It then rounds the hillside, turning south and converging with a lower track in the valley bottom.

The River Derwent accompanies the route for the rest of the walk, winding its way down the valley towards the reservoirs, the track eventually leading back to the bottom of the familiar Cranberry Clough. From there, its back over the boarded bridge, across the Slippery Stones bridge, and along the limestone track to King's Oak.

Route summary

Your present location	Your next objective	Waypoint at next objective	Directions
King's Oak terminus SK 16730 94050	Slippery Stones bridge	SK 16960 95120	Walking 1.5km north alongside the Derwent river
SK 16960 95120	Fork at marker post	SK 17040 95360	Go right (E) up the path marked 'Bridle Path'
SK 17040 95360	Fork in the path	SK 17520 95260	500m east. Go left (NE) at this fork
SK 17520 95260	Second of two cairns	SK 18580 96060	1.5km NE. Turn right (SSE) at the cairn towards Margery
SK 18580 96060	Margery pillar	SK 18911 95695	500m from the cairn
SK 18911 95695	Cairn	SK 18580 96060	Retrace your route back to the cairn
SK 18580 96060	Point on the path 180m SW of flying bomb site	SK 18440 96400	375m NNW (333 deg) from the cairn along Howden Edge
SK 18440 96400	Flying bomb explosion site	SK 18570 96520	180m NE across the grass moor
SK 18570 96520	Point on the path 180m SW of flying bomb site	SK 18440 96400	Retrace your route back to the main path
SK 18440 96400	Site of wreckage, Airspeed Oxford	SK 18040 96740	500m NW along the peat path
SK 18040 96740	Outer Edge pillar	SK 17703 96973	400m NW from the Airspeed Oxford
SK 17703 96973	Outer Edge Rocks	SK 17710 96880	100m due south from the pillar
SK 17710 96880	Site of wreckage, Airspeed Consul	SK 17410 96610	400m SW across the moor, past grouse butts
SK 17410 96610	Top of Broadhead Clough	SK 17540 96430	Walk SW to top of Crow Stones Edge, then turn SW. 300m total
SK 17540 96430	Stream crossing	SK 17120 96180	400m SW down Broadhead Clough
SK 17120 96180	Rejoin path coming down Cranberry Clough	SK 17040 95360	1km south along the valley track
SK 17040 95360	Slippery Stones bridge	SK 16960 95120	200m south, familiar ground
SK 16960 95120	King's Oak terminus	SK 16730 94050	Back to the start

Walk 5 – West End Moor, taking in Alport Castles

Start: Bridge End car park, on the west side of the Ladybower reservoir – Map reference SK 18000 88480

Distance: 19km (12 miles)

Total ascent: 540m (1750 ft)

Estimated time: 6 hours

Grading: Strenuous

OS map: Explorer map OL 1 The Peak District – Dark Peak area

The route

The route rises through the forest on the west side of the Ladybower reservoir, emerging on to open moorland above the Alport Castles rock formations. From there it follows the edge of Alport Dale, crossing the moor to the pillar before returning to the Castles and then descending to the reservoir road for the return leg.

The height profile shows a steady climb at the start, 8km of level walking on the moor, then a quick descent to the level of the reservoirs. The pillar is at the high point, but not on a pronounced peak.

The walk

Follow the track westwards from the south end of Bridge End car park, sign-posted to Crookhill, Rowlee and Lockerbrook. It rises steadily for 1km through the forest, turns NW and emerges on to open pastures at SK 17080 88500. At the stile gate, turn NW over Hagg Side and follow the edge of the forest for another 1km, reaching two tracks that merge as they intercept the route (at SK 16390 89030). Cross them both, taking the grass path on the far side that passes a notice board for 'Open Access Land'.

From there, follow the path, first NW, then north over the ladder stile at SK 16260 89170 on to Lockerbrook Heights. The walking is easy, the Snake Pass valley expanding below to the SW, with the A57 trunk road visible at the bottom. Eventually, an information board announces the area as being Rowlee Pasture, the terrain giving way to wet grass moorland. Fortunately, there is a 1.5km long stretch of paved path that provides easy walking towards Alport Castles. It was in the area of Rowlee Pasture that a Boulton Paul Defiant aircraft crashed in 1941, but it is possible that all the wreckage has since been removed. Often though, peat bog will swallow such debris, only to mysteriously release it again at a later

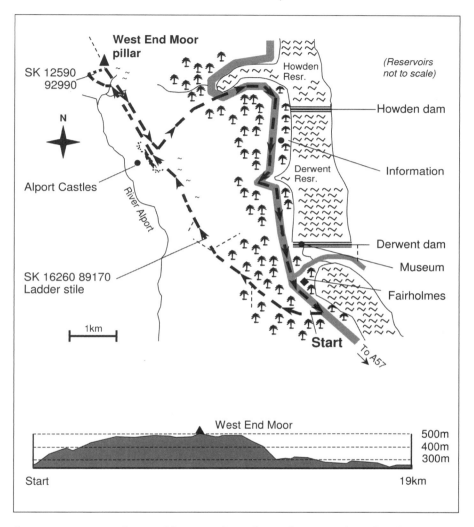

date. It is just one of several historical incidents that provide a ghostly aviation theme to this walk.

As the Snake Pass veers away to the west, the route turns north, following the edge of the Alport Dale valley. Before reaching Alport Castles, the paved path gives way to a wet peat track that skirts the remains of a wall. There, beware of deep holes or 'floating' patches of bog. At around SK 14650 91000, there are the first views of the 'Castle' formations, with the rock cliffs falling steeply into the valley and the prominent Tower Rock coming into sight. It's but a shadow of its

The first view of the Tower Rock

former self, the debris around the base bearing witness to the years of erosion. Looking down from the edge, the scene is 'pre-historic' in its dramatic beauty.

The rocks on Alport Castles are relatively soft shales, similar to those of Mam Tor and parts of The Roaches (further south in the Peak District). They are soft and unstable, liable to slippage, particularly after long periods of rain. It is suggested that the slippage at Alport Castles is the largest in England, and this can certainly be believed when viewed from the top. But that same instability means that the area is not a really popular rock-climbing venue, despite the challenging cliff formations.

The path that leaves to the NE from the Castles, at SK 14120 91670, will be the one to follow later in the walk, but before that, the route continues along the top of the valley, across Birchin Hat and on towards West End Moor. The views down into the Alport valley are splendid, with the river meandering along its path, marked by numerous waterfalls. It's in stark contrast to the dour landscape of the moorland scene to the east.

Upon reaching SK 13390 92600, the route crosses the first of two cloughs that run only 50m apart. At the second (SK 13350 92670), a path leaves to the NW, away from the edge, and actually goes to the pillar. But it's worth staying on the path along the edge, going west and then WNW, keeping the superb views of the valley until the last possible moment.

At SK 12590 92990, with the pillar 400m to the NE, look for a break in the peat overhangs to the right. This marks a shallow grough that can be negotiated for some distance whilst walking due NE towards the pillar. The precise compass bearing to follow is 049 deg, and as the grough runs out, look for the narrow path that walkers with the same idea have created. In fact, walking on top is not too difficult, often a good deal less wet than the well-walked path that the route eventually follows when leaving the trig point.

The West End Moor pillar survives intact, with its original plug and spider, but is generally waterlogged. It is possibly the most remote pillar in the Peak District.

The pillar details are:

Position: SK 12878 93255
Flush bracket No: S4298
Height: 503m (1,635 ft)
Horizon: 80km (50 miles)
Built: September 1947
Historic use: Secondary
Current use: None
Condition: Good

West End Moor pillar

The pillar triangulates with only eight others, the Kinder plateau cutting off views to the south and SW, and the Alport moor those to the NW. The views to the SE are a little more open, so that the very distant peaks with pillars at Stanage Edge and High Neb are just visible.

Pillar	Distance	Direction
Outer Edge (Howden)	6.1km	NENE (052 deg)
Margery Hill (Primary)	6.5km	ENE (068 deg)
Back Tor	7.2km	ESE (108 deg)
High Neb	12.7km	SESE (129 deg)
Stanage Edge	15.9km	SE (130 deg)
Edale Moor	5.4km	S (179 deg)
The Edge (Kinder, Primary)	6.5km	SWSW (233 deg)
Higher Shelf Stones *	4.3km	WNW (290 deg)

* The line of sight to Higher Shelf Stones is very marginal

From the pillar, follow the broad expanse of peat path that leaves to the SE, back towards the Castles; it's 600m of wet 'bog-hopping' to regain the edge of Alport Dale at the clough (SK 13350 92670). From there, return to the Castles, retracing the route along the edge. Ideally, the walk would have been a more complete loop, perhaps by walking NE across the Open Access land from the pillar and reaching Howden reservoir via Black Clough. There is even a tempting path leaving the pillar in that direction, but the terrain is very difficult, with any hint of the path soon disappearing. Black Clough itself is a rough descent, and entry into the forest is barred by high fences.

At SK 14120 91670, by the Castles, take the grassy path NE. It is a straightforward 2km walk past grouse butts into a wooded area around the reservoir inlet at Fox's Piece, west of the Howden dam. Before emerging on to the reservoir road, the path through the wood descends quite steeply, and the threat of slipping on fallen vegetation and tree roots is an obvious hazard.

Following the reservoir road east and south for 1.5km, the route passes Howden dam, which creates the Howden reservoir to its north. Along with the Derwent dam, which the route passes later to the south, it was built in the early 1900s. Between the two dams, which are set 2km apart, there are several information boards describing the history of their construction. Such was the scale of the project that a whole village sprang up ('Birchinlee', or 'Tin Town', as it was nick-named) to house the several hundred workforce and their families. It's long since gone, but the road itself is built on the foundations of the old railway track that was used to bring in the thousands of tonnes of constructional material. In late summer, if the water level is low enough, the remains of old wooden supports that carried the railway across the inlets emerge above the surface of the water.

Tribute to the Dambusters

At the Derwent dam there are several more information boards describing its construction. Further interesting history lies within in the western Turret, where there is a museum recalling the wartime exploits of the famous 617 Dambusters squadron. It exhibits photographs, memorabilia and a replica of the much renowned projectile designed by Barnes Wallace, the famous 'bouncing bomb'. During the second world war, the squadron practised low-level flying and bomb-aiming techniques on the approach to the Derwent dam, where the geography of the surrounding land and the twin turrets resembled the targets they were soon to confront in Germany. The museum, which is open Sundays and Bank Holidays, is well worth a visit.

With such history, it's not surprising that the 'spirit' of aviation has left its mark on the area. Ghostly apparitions have been reported over the reservoirs for numerous years, including one very strange incident in 1997, when a couple saw an aircraft flying at near ground level, disappearing behind the hills. They then heard the sound of an explosion and saw a huge flash in the sky. The emergency services were alerted, including a helicopter, mountain rescue and police with tracker dogs. But, after an extensive search, no trace of the aircraft was found. Local beliefs however, are that the aircraft was the ghost of a Lancaster bomber with the call sign "V for Vicky, the Vicious Virgin" which, having seen three years active service, had crashed on the moors during a routine flight. On that fatal flight in 1945, all six crew members had perished.

So, with those ghostly thoughts in mind, press on quickly for the last 1.5km, passing the Fairholmes visitor centre and regaining the car park on the west side of the road.

Route summary

Your present location	Your next objective	Waypoint at next objective	Directions
Start, Bridge End car park – SK 18000 88480	Point where the route emerges from the forest	SK 17080 88500	1km westwards, along the forest track
SK 17080 88500	Intersection of paths below Lockerbrook Heights	SK 16390 89030	1km NW, along the edge of the forest
SK 16390 89030	Ladder stile to enter Lockerbrook Heights	SK 16260 89170	200m NW from the intersection
SK 16260 89170	High point on Rowlee Pastures	SK 14810 90400	2km NW, along the moor path
SK 14810 90400	Above 'Tower Rock', with a path leaving NE (to be used later)	SK 14120 91670	1.5km generally NW, along the top of the ridge from Rowley
SK 14120 91670	First clough	SK 13390 92600	1.2km NW along the edge of Alport Dale
SK 13390 92600	Second clough, where the return path joins	SK 13350 92670	Only 50m NW from the first clough. Keep to the edge
SK 13350 92670	Break in the peat hags to the right (NE)	SK 12590 92990	800m NW from the clough, along the edge of Alport Dale
SK 12590 92990	West End Moor pillar	SK 12878 93255	400m NE across moor
SK 12878 93255	Back to the 'second clough' on the edge	SK 13350 92670	600m SE, along a boggy moor path
SK 13350 92670	Above 'Tower Rock'	SK 14120 91670	1.3km SE, along edge
SK 14120 91670	The reservoir road	SK 15470 92750	1.8km NE, across the moor and down through the forest
SK 15470 92750	Howden dam	SK 16820 92510	Follow the road for 1.5km east and then south
SK 16820 92510	Birchinlee	SK 16700 91700	1km south along the road from Howden dam
SK 16700 91700	Derwent dam	SK 17100 89780	1km south along the road from Birchinlee
SK 17100 89780	Car park	SK 18000 88480	1.5km south and then SE along the road

Walk 6 – Emlin Ridge and Kirk Edge

Start: On Smithy Bridge Road, by the memorial field, Centre of Low Bradfield – Map Reference SK 26360 91910

Distance: 14km (8.8 miles)

Total ascent: 510m (1657 ft)

Estimated time: 5 hours

Grading: Moderate

OS map: Explorer map OL 1 The Peak District – Dark Peak area

The route

The route makes use of public footpaths leading NE out of Low Bradfield, climbing to the pillar at Kirk Edge, where there is some curious astronomy equipment to examine. From there it proceeds westwards below Rocher Edge, taking in the Fundamental Benchmark pillar at Broomhead Moor, before visiting the pillar on Emlin Ridge and returning east to Low Bradfield.

The height profile shows a steep climb up to the Kirk Edge pillar, modest gradients in the middle section and a long descent at the end from the Emlin Ridge summit.

The walk

Before starting, take a moment to look across the memorial field. Dedicated to the Ibbotson family, who'd lived in Bradfield for some 20 generations, the field is at the centre of a thriving village life. There is no greater testimony to the spirit of

Village cricket and jousting in February!

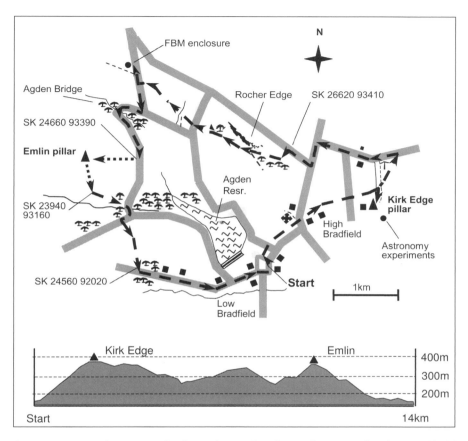

the community than to see both cricket and a show of jousting by the Bradfield Historical Society taking place on a cold February day!

The Ibbotsons played out their Lord of the Manor role for over 400 years from the mansion that overlooks the fields from the west, overseeing an essentially farming community. Now the village is more focused on the walking tourist, providing a network of numbered and well managed walking routes, preserving the delicate balance between the landscape and the needs of the farmer.

To begin the walk, proceed north along Smithy Bridge Road, keeping straight on along the limestone track (Sands Road) that leaves from the first right-hand bend. After 100m, at SK 26280 92080, where the track turns left over a stream, take the footpath off to the right, indicated as 'Footpath No 35'. Within 100m, a set of stone steps leads up to a wall stile and on to a path bordered by a wooden fence and a stone wall, eventually emerging on to a lane at SK 26350 92260.

Cross the lane, continuing through the wall gate on the other side, again marked as Footpath No 35.

The route then proceeds NE through grass pastures, following the remains of a stone wall where, after 200m, at SK 26530 92390, High Bradfield church comes into view. From that point, head towards the church itself, via the top corner of the field. The apparent path that leads lower in the field has been closed. From the top corner of the field, follow the left side of a wall, approaching the church through a wrought-iron gate at its SW corner. That leads to a path running the full length of the church grounds, behind a low castellated wall, emerging immediately outside the church gates.

The church of St Nicholas is a fine example of a 15th century Norman church, originally built in 1109 by the Lovetot family, Lords of the Manor under William the Conqueror's feudal system. The square bell-tower was added in the 14th century, before the church was enlarged and rebuilt in its current Gothic Perpendicular style during the 1480s. But it is really distinguished for its ancient Saxon cross, found buried in a field at Low Bradfield in 1870. Experts have dated the cross to the 9th century, two hundred years before the first stone was laid for the original church. For those interested, the church is well worth a visit, and booklets that tell of its historic past and that of the surrounding community can be purchased inside.

Walking on NE from the gates, into Jane Street, the route passes another historic building. This is the 'Watch House', built in 1831 to protect the cemetery from the grave robbers. Left unchecked, they could sell any number of fresh corpses to unscrupulous medical researchers. Continuing to the top of Jane Street, the route enters Round House Lane at SK 26770 92560. Take the stone stile immediately opposite, again following the footpath marker No 35. This is the start of a tree-lined avenue that continues for 200m, before emerging on to grass pastures via an exit set to the right of a farm gate. The path then continues 400m NE, following a wall and a sequence of stiles, across relatively level ground. At SK 27220 92850, it enters an area of Open Access land, the ground rising steeply for the next 150m before emerging on to a lane via a stile at SK 27440 92940.

On the other side of the lane, take the stile into the fields, again indicated as footpath No 35, walking briefly NE and then east across the field and up the hill towards a ladder stile at SK 27700 93030. There is no well-walked path, but it's an official right of way. From this ladder stile, the Kirk Edge pillar is visible some 100m to the right, but the path now veers NNE for 100m across the field to a fence stile at SK 27720 93100, accessing a partially metalled drive.

Turn right (south) along the drive and walk 200m, passing over a cattle grid into an area used by Sheffield University. Obviously derelict, it houses a curious selection of rusting astronomy equipment, relics of the research activities carried out by the Astronomy Department in the 1960s. The three tracking dishes stand silent, their rotating mechanisms exposed to the elements. Likewise, the buildings stand empty and neglected, and more equipment lies abandoned nearby.

The Kirk Edge pillar sits by a wall on the west side of the area, in front of the closed reservoir that serves the valley below. It's leaning a little, but otherwise in good condition, with the original OS plug, the spider and the flush bracket all in place.

Kirk Edge pillar

The pillar details are:

Position: SK 27723 92947
Flush bracket No: S2144
Height: 396m (1287 ft)
Horizon: 71km (44 miles)
Built: July 1938
Historic use: Secondary
Current use: None
Condition: Good

There is line-of-sight to around 18 local pillars from Kirk Edge, but many of them are in an urban area around the north of Sheffield, so the geography is difficult to assess, even with binoculars. Views to the south are good, but the extensive moors restrict visibility in the west. However, it's just possible to see Margery Hill and Outer Edge to the NW.

Leaving the pillar, retrace the route down the metalled drive to the stile in the east fence, at SK 27700 93110. Cross into the field and continue NE alongside a fence, crossing two stiles, the second (at SK 27930 93270) being so elaborate that it could be negotiated in high heels! From there, the path traverses open pastures, emerging over a wall stile on to a lane at SK 28020 93450. Turn left (west) and follow the lane for 1.2km to a T-junction, turning left again (south) and walking another 400m to the next junction. Go right (NW), and walk 350m to a stone stile by a gate on the left of the lane, this one marked 'Footpath No 119' (at SK 26620 93410).

The stile leads on to a grassy track, one that takes the route first south, and then turning steadily to a WNW heading as it drops down below the rocky escarpment of Rocher

Pillar	Distance	Direction
Champany Hill **	12.2km	NNNE (011 deg)
Greno Knoll	5.4km	NENE (060 deg)
Top End	5.1km	EENE (082 deg)
Birley Edge	5.4km	EESE (097 deg)
Shirecliffe Gunsite **	7.9km	ESE (114 deg)
Ringinglow	9.5km	SSSE (166 deg)
Ox Stones	9.8km	S (178 deg)
Stanage Edge	10.3km	SSSW (195 deg)
Rod Moor	4.7km	SSSW (198 deg)
High Neb	9.0km	WSSW (213 deg)
Winhill Pike *	11.9km	SW (229 deg)
Back Tor	8.1km	WWSW (256 deg)
Emlin Ridge	3.8km	WWNW (276 deg)
Margery Hill (Primary) *	9.2km	WNW (287 deg)
Outer Edge	10.7km	WNW (292 deg)
Whitwell Moor *	5.1km	WNNW (328 deg)
Hoyland Swaine	12.0km	NNNW (350 deg)
Hill Top Farm	6.2km	N (359 deg)

* The visibility to these pillars is marginal
** Pillar missing

Broomfield Moor Fundamental Bench Mark

Edge. At SK 26320 93270, the path descends a set of stone steps indicated by a marker post, steadily veering away from the Edge and dropping down to meet other paths joining from the left. Keep walking WNW to a ladder stile that bridges the wall on the left, at SK 26000 93360. Cross it, then turn immediately NW, ignoring a path and another ladder stile some 20m to the south.

The route then follows a well-walked track, signposted by regular markers, through a disused property at SK 25790 93500 on to a grass track. That runs for 500m, turning west after crossing a stream and emerging on to a lane at SK 25440 93770. Take the stile by the gate on the opposite side of the lane, the path then leading west over a boarded bridge and turning NW uphill towards a stone wall. Keeping to the right of the stone wall, follow the path briefly north, then NW for 1km across open moorland, emerging on to another lane at SK 24580 94500.

At this point there is a short 200m detour northwards (right) along the lane to visit the Broomfield Moor Fundamental Bench Mark pillar (FBM). It is secure within a protective cage on the roadside verge, still acting as an OS Passive Station. Whilst the cage is rusting, the pillar is sound, fitted with an OS plaque to warn against abuse. There is no flush bracket. It's shown as a small black circle on the Explorer OL1 map, and the location is typical, being off the beaten track, away from the normal haunts of vandals. The last recorded survey by the OS was in 2001, showing the height above sea level as 359.551m, but another survey is (or was) due in 2006.

From the FBM, retrace the route south, walking along the lane to a junction on a sharp right hand bend at SK 24780 94080. Keep right, following the road as it loops round the valley, crossing Agden Bridge and rising steeply on the other side, before turning south again. The access on to Bradfield Moor is at SK 24660 93390, identified by a gas marker-post positioned about ten metres from the lane.

From that point to the Emlin Ridge pillar is 700m on a 267 deg bearing (near due west). It's a hard slog across the heather moor, with a single low fence to step over just after the gas marker. The area is Open Access, but with restrictions, those relating to the grouse season and land management, so be vigilant for notices or stewards informing of any obligations, including the prohibition of dogs.

With a GPS, set the objective as SK 23987 93364 (the pillar), negotiating the heather as best you can. Burned patches often ease the way. In poor weather, with just a compass, it might be necessary to use the 'walk to' method referred to in the Introduction, but with the pillar on the high point, the principle of walking uphill should get you there.

The pillar has its original spider, insert and flush bracket, but is badly cracked around the base.

Emlin Ridge pillar

The pillar details are:

Position: SK 23987 93364
Flush bracket No: S4157
Height: 385m (1251 ft)
Horizon: 70km (44 miles)
Built: August 1947
Historic use: Secondary
Current use: None
Condition: Poor, cracked

Pillar	Distance	Direction
Kirk Edge	3.7km	EESE (096 deg)
Rod Moor	5.4km	SSE (155 deg)
Ox Stones *	11.0km	SSE (158 deg)
Stanage Edge *	10.4km	SSSE (174 deg)
High Neb *	8.1km	SSSW (188 deg)
Back Tor *	4.8km	SWSW (240 deg)

* The visibility to these pillars is marginal

The views to other pillars from Emlin Ridge are very poor, with only six in sight, and four of them are very marginal. The NE sector is blocked by White Lee Moor. Kirk Edge and Rod Moor obscure the Sheffield area, and Bradfield Moor itself restricts visibility to the SW. Margery Hill and Outer Edge, which are visible from Kirk Edge (because the line of sight is along the Agden valley) are not in view from Emlin, even though it's closer. Overall, it appears to be a redundant triangulation point.

The route off the moor back to the road is via a line of grouse butts, situated 150m to the SSW of the pillar (bearing 202 degrees), at SK 23940 93160. Walking downhill is easier, and the preparations for grouse shooting often mean that more of the heather has been cleared in that area. Once at the grouse butts, follow a clear vehicle track for 700m in a generally SE direction, to a gate at SK 24480 92760, then on for a further 100m to the lane.

Turn SE on the lane, walking 150m to a junction where another lane joins from the left. Ignoring that lane, continue for a further 40m south to a stile marker post at SK 24470 92600, identified as Footpath No 40. Over the stile, the path follows a wall SE down to a grass track that runs south, crossing open meadows, before emerging on to a lane at SK 24650 92020. 100m before the lane, the more obvious path diverts to the east, luring the unsuspecting walker off the correct route. Finally, once on the lane, turn left (east), following it for 1.8km back into Low Bradfield.

Route summary

Your present location	Your next objective	Waypoint at next objective	Directions
Smithy Bridge Rd SK 26360 91910	Footpath No 35, leading north	SK 26280 92080	North into Sands Road, then 100m to footpath
SK 26280 92080	Lane, cross it to follow path No 35	SK 26350 92260	250m, north and then NE, climbing steps
SK 26350 92260	First view of church	SK 26530 92390	200m NE. Then walk towards the church
SK 26530 92390	Church gates	SK 26740 92540	300m NE, up to and along castellated wall
SK 26740 92540	Round House Lane. Cross it to path No 35	SK 26770 92560	100m NE past the Watch House
SK 26770 92560	Lane, cross it and continue on path No 35	SK 27440 92940	750m NE then ENE along path with stiles
SK 27440 92940	Ladder stile, pillar visible 100m to the east	SK 27700 93030	250m ENE up the grassy slope
SK 27700 93030	Fence stile, leading on to metalled drive	SK 27720 93100	100m NNE, then turn right along the drive
SK 27720 93100	Kirk Edge pillar	SK 27723 92947	150m south, into the derelict area
SK 27723 92947	Fence stile on east side of the metalled drive	SK 27700 93110	Retrace your steps down the metalled drive
SK 27700 93110	Lane, where the route turns left (west)	SK 28020 93450	500m generally NE, over two stiles
SK 28020 93450	T-junction, turn left (S)	SK 26950 93500	1.2km west on the lane
SK 26950 93500	Y-junction, go right (NW)	SK 26880 93160	350m south
SK 26880 93160	Stone stile on left (S)	SK 26620 93410	350m NW, to path 119
SK 26620 93410	Stone steps, descending below Rocher Edge	SK 26320 93270	500m south, steadily turning WNW, on track
SK 26320 93270	Ladder stile, cross it and turn NW	SK 26000 93360	250m WNW from steps
SK 26000 93360	Disused property	SK 25790 93500	300m NW on path
SK 25790 93500	Lane, cross to stile on the other side	SK 25440 93770	500m NW and then north along a track
SK 25440 93770	Lane, where the route turns right	SK 24580 94500	1.1km NW, to right of wall, then across moor
SK 24580 94500	Broomfield FBM pillar	SK 24532 94651	200m north on lane
SK 24532 94651	Road junction, go right	SK 24780 94080	700m SSE on lane
SK 24780 94080	Access point to moor	SK 24660 93390	1.2km along the lane
SK 24660 93390	Emlin pillar	SK 23987 93364	700m west, bearing 267 deg across the moor
SK 23987 93364	Grouse butts	SK 23940 93160	150m SSW, bearing 202 deg
SK 23940 93160	Gate, then 100m to lane	SK 24480 92760	700m SE on track
SK 24480 92760	Stile, with marker post	SK 24470 92600	250m SW, then SE
SK 24470 92600	Gate to lane	SK 24650 92020	700m SSE along path
SK 24650 92020	Smithy Bridge Road	SK 26360 91910	1.8km east on lane

Walk 7 – Harry Hut, Cown Edge Rocks and Lantern Pike

Start: On a lay-by alongside the A624 trunk road, north of Hayfield – Map reference SK 03350 90900

Distance: 17km (10.6 miles)

Total ascent: 730m (2370 ft)

Estimated time: 6 hours

Grading: Strenuous

OS map: Explorer map OL 1 The Peak District – Dark Peak area

The route

The route crosses Chunal Moor to the Harry Hut pillar, drops down to the southern fringes of Glossop, before ascending via Whiteley Nab to Cown Edge. From there it crosses Mateley Moor on the way to Lantern Pike, before returning along the rural paths above Little Hayfield.

The height profile shows four significant ascents, so that the total climb is over 700m, making for a strenuous walk.

The walk

From the lay-by, take the wall stile at SK 03350 90900, following the path generally eastwards across the Open Access heather moor for 1.2km, up to the Harry Hut pillar. The sandstone path is clear and well walked, even though it doesn't appear on many maps. Half way, there is a ladder stile at SK 03900 90750. It's currently in a dangerous condition; use the gate to its right instead.

The Harry Hut pillar is in a sound condition, although the base is becoming exposed as erosion takes its toll. A stone plug has replaced the original OS insert, but the flush bracket and spider are intact.

The pillar details are:

Position: SK 04477 90771
Flush bracket No: S2781
Height: 441m (1433 ft)
Horizon: 75km (47 miles)
Built: May 1940
Historic use: Secondary
Current use: None
Condition: Good

Harry Hut pillar

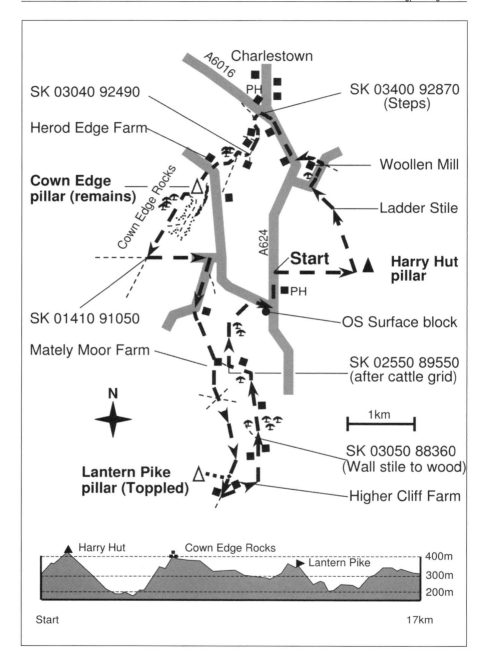

Charlestown

A6016

PH

SK 03040 92490

SK 03400 92870
(Steps)

Herod Edge Farm

Woollen Mill

**Cown Edge
pillar (remains)**

Cown Edge Rocks

Ladder Stile

A624

Start ▲ **Harry Hut
pillar**

SK 01410 91050

PH

OS Surface block

Mately Moor Farm

SK 02550 89550
(after cattle grid)

N

1km

**Lantern Pike
pillar (Toppled)**

SK 03050 88360
(Wall stile to wood)

Higher Cliff Farm

Harry Hut   Cown Edge Rocks

Lantern Pike   400m

300m

200m

Start   17km

Pillar	Distance	Direction
Featherbed Moss	10.4km	N (000 deg)
Holme Moss (Primary)	14.3km	NNNE (013 deg)
Cock Hill	5.6km	NNNE (014 deg)
Higher Shelf Stones	5.9km	NE (047 deg)
Burbage Edge	17.6km	S (184 deg)
Shining Tor	17.7km	SSSW (196 deg)
Sponds Hill	12.8km	WSSW (215 deg)
Nab Head *	15.8km	SW (221 deg)
Cown Edge Rocks **	2.6km	NWNW (298 deg)
Wild bank	9.1km	WNNW (322 deg)
Alphin Pike	12.7km	NNW (340 deg)

* Visibility to this pillar is marginal   ** Pillar missing

Visibility to nearby pillars is surprisingly restricted. Large areas of moorland block views from the NE round to the south, and there is no line-of-sight to the position of the Lantern Pike pillar, the third trig point in this walk. That is because that pillar was placed on the secondary peak, behind the higher Lantern Pike peak as viewed from Harry Hut. Shining Tor and Burbage Edge (Walk 17) are in view to the south, but nearly 18km distant.

From the pillar, follow the well-used path northwards through the heather, dropping down across Shaw Moor towards the Charlestown area of Glossop. After 700m, at SK 04280 91420, the route reaches the top of a rocky outcrop. It's a good place for refreshment, whilst admiring the extensive views across Whitethorn Clough to the east and Glossop to the north. A further 400m north from the outcrop, at SK 04130 91830, the path crosses a ladder stile and veers NW. Follow it downhill for 500m, across the moor to the lane below. Turn right, walking 400m along the lane to a drive on the left-hand side of the road, taking the route WNW through Gnat Hole Farm. The larger building at the rear of the farm is the old Gnat Hole woollen mill, believed to have been built in the first half of the eighteenth century. It's unusual for the area, since nearly all the local textile industry was based on cotton.

From the mill, follow the drive west up to the main road (A624), ignoring several paths that leave left and right. Cross the main road, turn right (NNW) and follow the pavement for 400m, approaching a fork in the road, with the Drover's Arms public house to the fore. At SK 03400 92870, ascend a flight of steps on the left, indicated by a footpath marker. They lead to a path that runs behind a row of properties, and then onwards to meet a limestone drive. It takes the route SW towards Herod Farm, passing Lees Hall on the way and eventually becoming a metalled road. Prior to reaching Herod Farm, on a sharp left-hand bend (at SK 03040 92490), a footpath leaves to the right, indicated to Whitley Nab. Take that path, climbing steeply NW for 100m through rough heather to a stile bordering open pastureland. From the stile, continue WSW over a further stile and up to a hole in the wall at SK 02710 92500.

There is a complex array of paths in this area, criss-crossing the route, so it's easy to make a mistake. Keeping on a WSW heading, follow the rutted track for only 50m from the hole in the wall. Then take the narrow path that branches to the right, aiming for a key waypoint at SK 02570 92480, a position by the east-facing corner of the tree plantation at Whiteley Nab. From there, the path skirts the southern edge of the trees for 200m, before leading on to a field track.

The track takes the route across a stile, up to a shingle drive below Herod Edge Farm. To the side of the farm are two stiles, take the one furthest left, leading through an area of rough pasture, emerging on to a lane (Monk's Road) at SK 02200 92250.

On the other side of the lane, a stile marks the path leading up to Cown Edge Rocks, bordered each side by range-wire fencing. At the top, two metres to the east side of the east fence at SK 02156 92038, is the site of the missing pillar. The position is 11 posts along from where the fenced path widens out at the top, after the steep ascent. All that remains of the pillar is a few fragments of concrete. To enter the Open Access area where the pillar had been situated, use the stile 100m further south along the fence and walk back.

A walking book dated 1982 shows the pillar intact, but it is known to have been absent by 1987. So sometime during that period it was broken up, probably vandalised.

The pillar details were:

Position: SK 02156 92038
Flush bracket No: Lost (was S2639)
Height: 411m (1336 ft)
Horizon: 72km (45 miles)
Built: July 1939
Historic use: Secondary
Current use: None
Condition: Destroyed (1982/87)

From the site there are good views north and NE to Cock Hill, Higher Shelf Stones, Featherbed Moss and the Primary pillar at Holme Moss. Except for Harry

A few fragments of the Cown Edge Rocks pillar

Hut, visibility to pillars in the east is poor, but to the south, Chinley Churn is in view, as is the pillar position on the second-ary Lantern Pike peak, the line not being ob-scured by the main peak. From the SW round to the NW there would have been excellent triangula-tion to at least ten pillars in the region of Stock-port, Manchester and Oldham, and it's proba-ble that the Cown Edge Rocks position would have been a key reference point for some of the urban surveying. However, those views are now restricted by the tree plantation on the NW of the ridge.

Continuing the walk, leave the pillar SSW, following the path for 250m between the two fences down to a gate and stile. After a further 100m SW, at SK 02040 91750, the well-walked path begins to descend, ultimately passing below the rocky outcrops. Don't follow it down, instead, turn briefly west through the rock formations (an old quarry), climbing the other side to gain the flatter ground on the top of the ridge. From there, follow the path SW for 300m, aiming for the southerly corner of the plantation on the west side of the ridge, at SK 01730 91550. Then cross the stile gate and continue SW along the sandstone track for another 600m. The walking is excellent.

At SK 01410 91050, cross the next stile gate and turn due east down a rutted sandstone track. It drops down to a stile that exits on to a made road, emerging after 1km through a gate (indicating 'Cown Edge Farm') and then continuing for a further 50m to the corner of a lane (SK 02320 90990). Turn right and follow the lane, indicated 'No Through Road', SSW for 500m to a point where it turns sharp right (SK 02200 90470). There, cross the stile in the south wall, on to the Open Access area of Matley Moor.

The path south across the moor is well used, emerging through a wall gate on to a sandstone drive at SK 02150 90080. Follow the drive SSE for 500m up to Matleymoor Farm (SK 02400 89560), where the path onwards becomes a limestone track, flanked by stone walls. It runs south for another 700m, before reaching an intersection of six paths (at SK 02530 88950). Pass through the gate on the right (west) and follow the bridle-path across the rough pasture, keeping on a SSE bearing. At any time of the year, you may encounter one of the more hardy breeds of long-horn cattle on these pastures. They may look formidable, but in general they seem very placid animals.

After 500m, at SK 02670 88500, in the far corner of the field, pass through the stile gate (marked 'Bridleway – No Vehicles'), walking up the steep sandstone track for 100m to the National Trust Sign for Lantern Pike. Go right there, up the diagonal path through the heather, reaching the toposcope on the main summit after 300m. From there, the views easterly into the Kinder basin and

I'm watching you!

NE to Bleaklow are excellent. To the SW is the lower of the two Lantern Pike summits, the next objective on the route.

Leaving the toposcope, continue SSW along the path, walking 230m to a point at SK 02550 87940. Turn right there, following a faint path through the heather for 50m towards a low wall and fence at the bottom. Step over the wall at its lowest point and climb the hill on the other side towards the toppled pillar. Both sides of the wall are Open Access, so there are no trespassing issues.

The pillar is lying on its side on the sloping ground, some 25m east from its original position (which was SK 02375 87961), due west on the top of the hill. The records show that it was vanda-lised in 1965, and abandoned by the OS as lost. The flush bracket and spider were removed.

The pillar details were:

Position: SK 02375 87961
Flush bracket No: Lost (was S2779)
Height: 359m (1169ft)
Horizon: 68km (42 miles)
Built: November 1940
Historic use: Secondary
Current use: None
Condition: Toppled (1965)

Lantern Pike pillar

The reason for positioning the pillar on the lower Lantern Pike peak remains a mystery. The views are inferior to those from the main summit, and there are no additional pillar sites in view that couldn't have been seen from the higher peak. When erected, it would have triangulated with about 10 pillars, mainly on the western side, duplicating many of those visible from Cown Edge rocks.

To continue, retrace the route over the fence and back to the main path (at SK 02550 87940). Turn right there (south), walk 100m down to a wall, turn left (east) and follow it down to the sandstone track. Pass through the gate on the right, fol-lowing the track SW for 300m to a drive on the left-hand side (at SK 02460 87600), marked by iron gates and a cattle grid, with a sign indicating 'High Cliff Farm'. Turn left on to the drive, following it for 200m, then leaving it to skirt around the south side of the farm, finally emerging into open pastures.

At this point on the walk, because the paths are vague, navigation can be a lit-tle tricky. 100m east from the house there is a stile, just through a gate on the left, at SK 02740 87680. It's easy to miss. Cross it and continue east, over a second stile only 40m further on. From that stile, the route continues east, following a stone wall downhill before veering NE into a well-trodden gully, leading to a third stile at SK 03040 87830. That is a key waypoint, and leads on to a narrow earth track skirted by a thorn hedge on the right. It can be very muddy, but after 100m it emerges on to a hard drive.

With Little Hayfield visible in the valley to the right, follow the drive northwards for 400m, passing through a gate by Cliff Bank Farm and then climbing steeply up a rutted path. After 100m, turn right over a wall stile, taking the path that continues north for 700m through a section of woodland, emerging on the other side into open pastures. The path reaches a metalled drive, leading quickly to a road crossing west to east, at SK 02950 09050 (Brookhouses).

Turn right there, following the road downhill for 100m, passing several properties and then turning left into the lane marked as being a 'No Through Road'. Follow it for 800m in a generally NW direction, passing Stet Farm and Lane Head Farm, to a cattle grid just before a sharp left hand turning (at SK 02550 89550). From the bend, take the rough track that leaves to the right (north), following it NNE for 600m, over two stiles, as it becomes a rutted grass path, finally emerging on to a farm drive at SK 02730 90190. From there, it is 300m NE down to the lane (Monk's Road), where the route turns right towards the A624 main road.

About 20m before the main road, look for a field gate in the fence on the south side of the lane. One metre in front of the centre of the gate (SK 03225 90260), set into the ground, is the OS 'Hollingworth Head Surface Block'. It's a concrete block, about 50cm square, with a small bolt in the centre. You may have to prod the ground to find it, or even cut away some grass. It is a typical position for one of these blocks, by a quiet country lane where it's unlikely to be disturbed, and easily accessible. However, the gate is not present on the original OS records (sketch and photograph), so it must be a recent addition, meaning that the block may have been disturbed by farm traffic.

The OS records show it as a Passive Station, last surveyed in 1998 and due for another visit in 2008. Its co-ordinates are very accurately determined. For instance, the elevation is quoted as the 'ETRS89 Geodetic Ellipsoid height', at 382.090m (that is a precision of one millimetre!), as well as the 'Orthometric height above mean sea level', at 331.243m. The latter is the British National Grid system, agreeing

Surface block

well with nearby spot heights on the OS maps and with the authors' GPS reading at the site, that was 333m elevation. As explained in the Introduction, the ETRS89 ellipsoid is a best fit for the entire earth, producing a significant error in the sea level height for this position in the UK (near 50m error). When the block is next surveyed, it will reveal the very small movements in the position and height of that part of the UK that have occurred over the preceding ten years.

Finally, to complete the route, there is 700m of walking northwards along the main road back to the lay-by, passing a tempting public house on the way!

Route summary

Your present location	Your next objective	Waypoint at next objective	Directions
Lay-by on A624, SK 03350 90900	Ladder stile and gate	SK 03900 90750	600m east across the heather moor
SK 03900 90750	Harry Hut pillar	SK 04477 90771	600m east from stile
SK 04477 90771	Rocky outcrop, Shaw Moss	SK 04280 91420	700m NNW downhill across the moor
SK 04280 91420	Ladder stile, then veer NW	SK 04130 91830	400m NNW
SK 04130 91830	Lane	SK 03750 92120	500m NW, downhill
SK 03750 92120	Drive, Gnat Hole Farm	SK 04060 92360	400m NE along the lane
SK 04060 92360	A624 main road	SK 03570 92510	500m W along drive
SK 03570 92510	Flight of stone steps	SK 03400 92870	400m NNW, path marker on the left
SK 03400 92870	Left-hand bend, with path marker to Whitley on right	SK 03040 92490	Up steps to drive, then 500m SW along drive
SK 03040 92490	Hole in wall	SK 02710 92500	300m, first WNW, then WSW over two stiles
SK 02710 92500	East corner of plantation – **Key Waypoint**	SK 02570 92480	150m WSW, complex paths
SK 02570 92480	Monk's Road (lane)	SK 02200 92250	400m SW, past farm
SK 02200 92250	Cown Edge pillar site	SK 02156 92038	200m S, between fences
SK 02156 92038	Old quarry, go right to keep on top of ridge	SK 02040 91750	350m S and SW from pillar site
SK 02040 91750	Southern corner of plantation, stile to fore	SK 01730 91550	300m SW, path across pastureland, cross the stile
SK 01730 91550	Stile gate	SK 01410 91050	1km SW along the top
SK 01410 91050	Lane, go right	SK 02320 90990	1km W down drive
SK 02320 90990	Right bend, take stile in wall	SK 02200 90470	600m SSW along lane
SK 02200 90470	Sandstone drive	SK 02150 90080	400m south across moor
SK 02150 90080	Matleymoor Farm	SK 02400 89560	500m SSE
SK 02400 89560	Six way path crossing, take gate on right	SK 02530 88950	700m south
SK 02530 88950	Stile gate	SK 02670 88500	500m south, bridle path
SK 02670 88500	Lantern Pike toposcope	SK 02610 88180	150m S, to the summit
SK 02610 88180	Point to go right to fallen pillar	SK 02550 87940	230m SSW along the top
SK 02550 87940	Fallen Lantern Pike pillar	SK 02400 87960	200m west from main path, stepping over a wall
SK 02400 87960	Rejoin main path	SK 02550 87940	200m east, back again
SK 02550 87940	Drive to High Cliff Farm	SK 02460 87600	400m, south, then ESE to gate, then SW on lane
SK 02460 87600	Stile (easy to miss)	SK 02740 87680	100m east of farm
SK 02740 87680	Stile to narrow earth track — **Key Waypoint**	SK 03040 87830	400m east, then NE. Earth track leads to a drive
SK 03040 87830	Wall stile, path to wood	SK 03050 88360	600m N, along drive, then steep path
SK 03050 88360	Lane, go south	SK 02950 09050	700m N from wall stile
SK 02950 09050	Track to right, after cattle grid	SK 02550 89550	1.1km total, loop S, then N, then NE along lane
SK 02550 89550	Monk's Road (lane)	SK 02900 90400	900m NNE, from cattle grid, path and farm drive
SK 02900 90400	OS Surface Block	SK 03225 90260	400m ESE, near gate
SK 03225 90260	Lay-by	SK 03350 90900	700m north along A624

Walk 8 – Back Tor, taking in Derwent Edge

Start: At the Fairholmes visitor centre, 400m south of the Derwent dam – Map reference SK 17200 89300

Distance: 13km (8.1 miles)

Total ascent: 440m (2080 ft)

Estimated time: 4.5 hours

Grading: Moderate

OS map: Explorer map OL 1 The Peak District – Dark Peak area

The route

The route passes in front of the Derwent dam, follows the east side of the Derwent reservoir, then climbs Abbey Bank before crossing the Green Sitches moor to Lost Lad and the Back Tor pillar. The route continues south along Derwent Edge, prior to dropping down to the Ladybower reservoir and finally turning north back to the dam and the Fairholmes centre.

The height profile shows the steep ascent up to the pillar, reasonably level walking along Derwent Edge, and a gentle descent back to the reservoir.

The walk

From Fairholmes, walk NE, passing in front of the Derwent dam, then climb the set of stone steps by the eastern turret, leading up to the track that follows the east side of Derwent reservoir. When the reservoir is in full flood, water cascading over the dam between the two turrets provides a superb spectacle. Once on the east side of the reservoir, follow the track north for 1km to SK 17370 90900. There, leaving the water's edge, turn eastwards along a footpath signposted to Bradfield and Strines. The path crosses a stile gate and then zigzags steeply upwards through the ferns in a generally NE direction.

At SK 17650 91170 another path crosses the route; keep straight on (east), continuing for 1km on to Green Sitches moor. There, the path divides (at SK 18390 91100). Take the left fork to the NE, following the path for a further 1km and climbing steeply up to Lost Lad. From the top, a panoramic view unfolds, including Howden Moor and Margery Hill to the north, Bleaklow to the NW, Kinder to the east and Winhill to the south. There is a toposcope indicating the various peaks and points of interest around the horizon.

From Lost Lad, follow the paved path SE across the peat moor for 500m, up to the rock formation that marks the Back Tor peak, with the pillar perched in a commanding position on the very top. Back Tor is just one of the striking rock formations that are encountered along the edge.

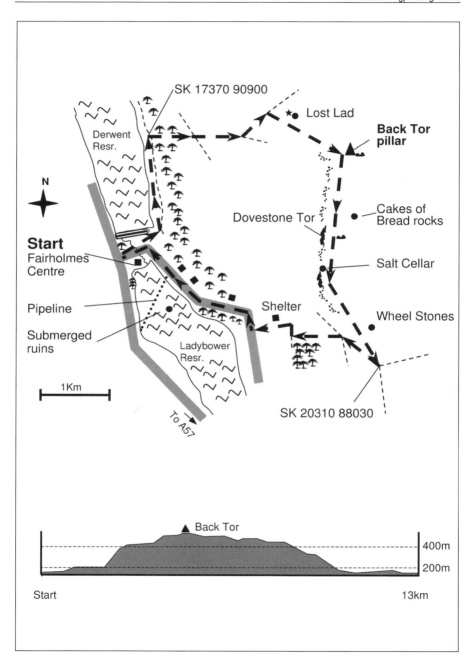

SK 17370 90900

Lost Lad

Back Tor pillar

Derwent Resr.

N

Dovestone Tor

Cakes of Bread rocks

Salt Cellar

Start
Fairholmes Centre

Pipeline

Submerged ruins

Shelter

Wheel Stones

Ladybower Resr.

1Km

To A57

SK 20310 88030

Back Tor

400m

200m

Start

13km

Back Tor pillar is in good condition, painted white, but with the OS plug replaced with a plastic insert. To reach and touch it requires a little rock climbing across the gritstone formations.

The pillar details are:

Position: SK 19763 90991
Flush bracket No: S2145
Height: 538m (1748 ft)
Horizon: 83km (52 miles)
Built: July 1938
Historic use: Secondary
Current use: None
Condition: Good

Back Tor pillar

From Back Tor, some 16 local pillars are in sight, but these don't include Margery Hill and Outer Edge, sites that are only about 6km north. They are obscured by the flat top of Howden moor. Visibility east and south is excellent, with the two pillars on Stanage Edge (Stanage and High Neb) both in view, as well as the distant Sir William Hill, with its distinctive communication mast. Due south is Winhill Pike and SW is Mam Tor.

Pillar	Distance	Direction
Whitwell Moor *	8.1km	ENNE (039 deg)
Emlin Ridge *	4.8km	NENE (060 deg)
Kirk Edge	8.1km	EENE (076 deg)
Loxley Common	11.2km	E (091 deg)
Rod Moor	6.9km	ESE (112 deg)
Ox Stones	11.4km	SE (134 deg)
Stanage Edge	9.5km	ESSE (146 deg)
High Neb *	6.4km	SSE (152 deg)
Sir William Hill	13.2km	SSSE (172 deg)
Abney Moor	11.7km	SSSW (188 deg)
Winhill Pike	6.0km	SSSW (190 deg)
Bradwell Moor	12.7km	WSSW (211 deg)
Mam Tor	10.2km	SW (223 deg)
Edale Moor *	7.5km	WSW (245 deg)
West End Moor	7.3km	WNW (288 deg)
Higher Shelf Stones	11.5km	WNW (289 deg)

* The visibility to these pillars is marginal

Looking south from the vantage point on Back Tor rocks, the ongoing route along Derwent Edge is marked by a long paved path, leading towards a series of unusual rock formations.

The first to be encountered are 'The Cakes of Bread', situated just to the east of the path near SK 19800 90100, a line of eroded rock piles that are indeed 'bread-like' in appearance. Walking on a further 400m, the next rock formation is Dovestone Tor, with one gritstone 'table-like' feature that is surely in danger of sliding off its plinth. A further 700m south, positioned on the edge of the outcrop overlooking the Derwent Valley, is the distinctive 'Salt Cellar', very aptly named from its shape. Finally, as the path continues south for another 1km, and then begins to turn SE, the impressive 'Wheel Stones' formation comes into view.

Cakes of Bread rock formations

The common feature of all these rock formations is relentless erosion, over thousands of years. The coarse gritstone rocks were laid down millions of years ago as progressive layers of sediment washed down to a prehistoric continental shelf. Compressed by the weight above, the sediments eventually became thick rock strata, before being lifted from the sea by movements in the earth's crust. But the deposition was spasmodic, with occasional changes in the climate producing softer layers in the sequence. And now it is those softer layers that are preferentially eroded, the relentless wind, rain and frost chiselling out the rock and revealing the layered structure. But it will take as long to erode them as it did to produce them. Take another photograph of the Wheel Stones ten years from now and you won't be able to see the difference.

From the Wheel Stones, continue SSE for 500m to SK 20310 88030, where the route turns right (NW) at a public footpath post. The path descends diagonally (NW) for 500m, joining a lower path. Follow that path for 50m to a gap in the wall at SK 19800 88410, signposted to Derwent. There, the path turns due west and descends for another 700m, skirting an area of woodland. At SK 19090 88390, the route turns NNW and then west along a cobbled section of path down to some recently renovated stone buildings. They can provide a welcome refuge in poor weather. Inside, there are some interesting contributions of drawings and poetry by the children of Bamford Primary School.

From there, it is 300m down a grass path to the road that runs alongside the Ladybower reservoir. Follow that road NW for 1.8km, back towards the Derwent dam, pausing to read the information boards on the way. They tell of the Derwent

Wheel Stones

and Ashopton villages, submerged when the Ladybower reservoir was created, the residents relocated to the surrounding communities and the graves in the Derwent churchyard moved to Bamford. But the church steeple itself remained stubbornly above the water, a testimony to the drowned village below, until it was deemed unsafe and was destroyed. And the old packhorse bridge, which crossed the River Derwent in the village centre, was relocated to the top end of Howden reservoir at Slippery Stones, where it still stands today.

But even now, when the reservoir level is very low, there are tantalising glimpses of the old foundations, the remains of Derwent village showing briefly above the water (just south of the pipeline) and reminding us of the communities lost forever.

Route summary

Your present location	Your next objective	Waypoint at next objective	Directions
Fairholmes Centre SK 17200 89300	Top of steps on east side of dam	SK 17490 89860	Cross in front of the dam
SK 17490 89860	Footpath leaving east to Bradfield and Strines	SK 17370 90900	1km north along the reservoir's edge
SK 17370 90900	Point where a path crosses the route, SE-NW	SK 17650 91170	400m NE up the steep incline; keep straight on at the crossing
SK 17650 91170	Fork in path on Green Sitches moor	SK 18390 91100	800m generally east; go left at the fork
SK 18390 91100	Top of Lost Lad	SK 19340 91200	1km from the fork
SK 19340 91200	Back Tor pillar	SK 19763 90991	500m SE from Lost Lad
SK 19763 90991	Passing by the Cakes of Bread rocks	SK 19800 90100	800m south from the pillar
SK 19800 90100	Dovestone Tor	SK 19700 89810	400m south from Cakes of Bread
SK 19700 89810	Passing Salt Cellar rock	SK 19660 89280	700m south from Dovestone Tor
SK 19660 89280	Passing Wheel Stones	SK 20200 88490	1km SE from Salt Cellar
SK 20200 88490	Path cross roads, turn right (west)	SK 20310 88030	500m SSE from Wheel Stones
SK 20310 88030	Gap in the wall, signposted to Derwent	SK 19800 88410	500m NW down the hill from the crossing
SK 19800 88410	Path turns NNW	SK 19090 88390	700m west, skirting woodland
SK 19090 88390	Stone refuge, with poetry displays	SK 18950 88470	200m NNW and west down the slope
SK 18950 88470	Meet the road alongside Ladybower Reservoir	SK 18720 88390	300m from the refuge, down the grass path
SK 18720 88390	Road below Derwent Dam	SK 17300 89630	1.8km along the water's edge
SK 17300 89630	Fairholmes Centre	SK 17200 89300	Back to the start

Walk 9 – The Edge and Kinder Low

Start: At the Kinder Road car park – Map reference SK 04800 86900

Distance: 12.7km (8.0 miles)

Total ascent: 640m (2080 ft)

Estimated time: 5 hours

Grading: Moderate to strenuous

OS map: Explorer map OL 1 The Peak District – Dark Peak area

The route

The route skirts Kinder Reservoir, follows William Clough to its source, then turns SE up to the Kinder plateau, passing some aircraft wreckage, before continuing along the west edge. There is a short excursion across the moor to reach The Edge pillar, before returning to the edge path, walking around Kinder Downfall and visiting the Kinder Low pillar. The route back is via the Kinder Low burial ground and down across open pastureland to the car park.

The height profile shows the steep ascent and descent, with the period of level walking on top. Both pillars are above 620m.

The walk

Before leaving the car park, take a look at the commemorative plaque set on the rock face at the back. It marks an important event, one that paved the way for the walking privileges that we all enjoy today.

The route follows that taken by one of the groups in the great mass trespass of 1932, when hundreds of ramblers set off to walk across Kinder Scout and the surrounding areas. Their point was one of principle, that any person should be allowed to enjoy the beauty of the open hills and moorland without the threat of prosecution from the private landowners.

They set off from three separate starting points, the aim being to divide any opposition. Those from Hayfield walked from the Kinder Road car park area, skirted Kinder Reservoir and climbed William Clough. The Hope group approached via Jacob's Ladder and the third party came along what is now the Pennine Way, from the high point on the A57 Snake Pass. The nominated meeting area was at Ashop Head.

The landowners recruited extra gamekeepers to confront what they saw as a blatant provocation, leading to several major skirmishes, particularly at the top of William Clough. But the keepers were heavily outnumbered, and the three parties converged unchecked for their victory meeting at Ashop Head. From there, all the ramblers returned to Hayfield, where the police allowed them a victory parade into the town. Once in the town, however, the march was halted

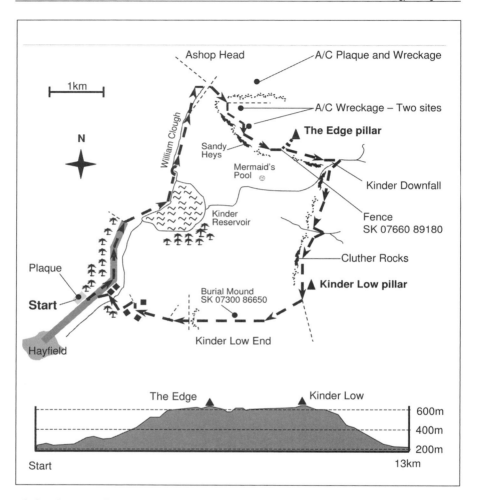

whilst the gamekeepers identified the ringleaders, and five men were plucked from the crowd by the police and arrested.

It was a hollow gesture; an important precedent had been set for the freedom to ramble, one that eventually led to large amounts of land being opened to the public, something we now take for granted.

To start the walk, leave the car park and follow the Kinder Road in a NE direction, ignoring the road that leaves to the right. After 900m, the road reaches a gate marking the entrance to Water Board property. Go though it, following the signpost marked 'Concession bridleway to Kinder reservoir' until reaching a set of locked gates (SK 05280 88000). Take the stile gate to the left and follow the cobbled path. It's an old mule track, the cobbles giving the animals extra grip as they laboured up the steep gradient. They also provide the same luxury for walkers, but, after 200m, the cobbles give way to a normal gritstone path. It skirts the NW side of the Kinder reservoir for 800m, eventually reaching a stone-walled bridge at the bottom of William Clough (SK 05930 88740). The reservoir itself is fairly modest in size, serving Hayfield and the surrounding area.

The walk up the clough is 1.5km, with a 200m ascent. The path is spasmodic, crossing and re-crossing the clough several times, with one or two tricky areas. It's a little hard on the feet in places, but the stiff climb at the top is made easier by a sequence of stone steps. At SK 06190 89710, an alternative path forks to the right and takes to the higher ground on the east side of the clough. It's best to ignore that path, walking alongside (or sometimes in) the clough, eventually keeping to its west side.

At the top (SK 06320 90170), follow the paving stones east, across the source area of William Clough, eventually joining the Pennine Way. The route then turns SE, rising very steeply up to the NW side of the Kinder plateau. Looking back from the top, there is a good view of the path that leads to Mill Hill in the West, as well as the Snake Path as it follows Ashop Clough towards the east.

Once on the top, the gritstone path takes the route along the SW side of Kinder, towards the Downfall. At numerous locations to the east of the path are the scattered remnants of two Sabre jets that crashed in 1953. For instance, there is wreckage at SK 06960 89710, SK 07030 89730 and SK 07080 89420 (that last area being very near the path, off Sandy Heys). Making a wider exploration of the area around those three locations should reveal further remnants of the aircraft. In fact, more wreckage is to be found on Black Ashop Moor, below Kinder north face at SK 07280 90270, where there is a memorial for the two pilots who died, and at SK 07350 90250, where there are the remains of a jet engine.

Anyone moving well east off the path to look for wreckage is advised to regain the edge path rather than attempting any direct bearing to The Edge pillar. The area is very difficult walking. Instead, follow the edge path round to a point by a fence (SK 07660 89180), then head due north back uphill. It is 300m to the pillar from the path at that point.

The Edge pillar is a Primary, one of the first 300 triangulation points to be established. But, as will be evident at the site, the original pillar has fallen (in 1944), presumably as the surrounding peat was lost to erosion, and a replacement pillar was erected (in June 1945). If it had been a Secondary pillar, that step would probably not have been taken. The new pillar is in excellent condition, painted white, but with the OS plug replaced with a plastic insert. There is no 'S' with the flush bracket number, typical of a Primary pillar.

The pillar details are:

Position: SK 07698 89370
Flush bracket No: 3443 (Number on the 1936 original, unknown)
Height: 625m (2031 ft)
Horizon: 89km (56 miles)
Built: April 1936, replaced June 1945
Historic use: Primary
Current use: None
Condition: Good

The Edge pillar

Surprisingly, from The Edge there is line-of-sight to only nine local pillars, so it is not one of the best Primary sites. Views east round to south are all restricted by the flat top of the Kinder plateau itself, which cuts off the views to Edale Moor, Winhill Pike and Mam Tor. The same problem restricts views to the NW towards Harry Hut and Cown Edge Rocks (missing).

Taking a more distant perspective reveals that it has views to five other Primaries, including Rivington, which is by the Winter Hill transmitter NW of Manchester.

Pillar	Distance	Direction
Higher Shelf Stones	5.5km	NNNE (012 deg)
Outer Edge	12.6km	NENE (052 deg)
West End Moor	6.5km	NENE (053 deg)
Margery Hill (Primary)	12.8km	NENE (060 deg)
Back Tor	12.1km	EENE (082 deg)
Kinder Low	2.3km	SSSE (174 deg)
Ladder Hill	11.6km	SSW (205 deg)
Chinley Churn	7.1km	WSSW (215 deg)
Sponds Hill	13.9km	SW (229 deg)

From the pillar, retrace your steps to the SW edge path and continue generally south-easterly for 800m to the Kinder Downfall, where the Kinder River cascades over the edge on its course to supply the reservoir below. To cross the river, follow it upstream for about 100m and then come back west on the other side. (Continuing east up-stream from there takes ramblers along 'Kinder Gates' and into the heart of the plateau; a very challenging walking area. It was the old route of the Pennine Way, crossing to Grinds Brook on the Edale side).

Viewed from either side, the Downfall rock formations are dramatic, and if there's a strong SW wind blowing, channelled into the mouth of the gully, there is the additional spectacle of blown spray carrying for hundreds of metres back on to the plateau. Sometimes, it seems that little or no water actually makes it over the falls. In cold, still conditions, the same waterfall produces spectacular ice formations, creating some very challenging ice-climbs for the enthusiasts.

Continuing south along the edge, after about 300m it's worth a look west at the moorland below to pick out a small pool located some 500m below the Downfall. It's known as 'Mermaid's Pool', and abounds with myth and legend. One story goes that a mermaid bathes in the moonlight on Easter Eve, and any person who sees her will become immortal!

From there, continue for 1.5km along the edge, walking SSW, over Red Brook, along the top of Cluther Rocks and up to the point (SK 07800 87400) where the path veers SSE towards the Kinder Low pillar. There is more than one path along the edge, but the area is so well walked that it

Downfall spray

hardly matters which one you use.

The Kinder Low pillar is perched on top of some very interesting gritstone rock formations, surrounded by a barren area of peat and stones. In fact, all three pillar sites on Kinder are so well frequented that vegetation of any kind around the pillars quickly falls victim to the walking boot. The pillar is in good condition, painted white, but with the OS plug replaced with a stone insert.

The pillar details are:

Position: SK 07904 87059
Flush bracket No: S4113
Height: 633m (2057 ft)
Horizon: 90km (56 miles)
Built: July 1947
Historic use: Secondary
Current use: None
Condition: Good

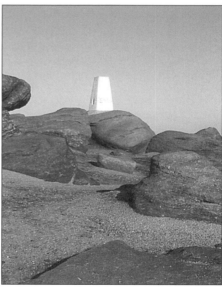

The visibility from the pillar is excellent, with at least 19 other pillars in sight, including those around the east and south that could not be seen from The Edge pillar. Brown Knoll pillar is only 2km south from Kinder Low, so it appears that the Kinder Low pillar may have been added between that and The Edge to make up for the inadequate triangulations from the Primary site. (The three pillars lie nearly on a straight line, roughly north-south, the

Kinder Low pillar

Kinder Low pillar post-dating the other two by seven years). It's clear that a flat-topped peak (like The Edge), irrespective of the elevation, is not the most ideal site for a pillar.

Leave Kinder Low pillar on a SW heading (235 deg), making the objective as the ancient burial ground at SK 07300 86650; it is 700m distant. (On the older maps, it will be marked as a cairn, but that has now been removed). The area immediately around the pillar is open walking, before leading on to grass moor. After 200m there is a paved path, but it may be necessary to

Pillar	Distance	Direction
Higher Shelf Stones	7.8km	NNNE (007 deg)
Edale Moor *	5.1km	EENE (081 deg)
High Neb *	15.0km	EESE (096 deg)
Winhill Pike	10.9km	EESE (100 deg)
Stanage Edge	17.6km	EESE (103 deg)
Flask Edge	22.1km	ESE (112 deg)
White Edge	21.5km	SESE (121 deg)
Sir William Hill	16.4km	SESE (124 deg)
Mam Tor	5.9km	SESE (125 deg)
Abney Moor	12.6km	SESE (127 deg)
Brown Knoll	2.0km	SSSE (167 deg)
Black Edge	10.2km	SSSW (189 deg)
Ladder Hill	9.6km	WSSW (212 deg)
Chinley Churn	5.5km	SWSW (232 deg)
Sponds Hill	12.8km	SWSW (238 deg)
Cobden Edge	9.2km	W (271 deg)
Lantern Pike **	5.6km	WWNW (280deg)
Cown Edge Rocks ***	7,6km	NW (310 deg)
Harry Hut *	5.1km	NW (317 deg)

* The visibility to these pillars is marginal ** Pillar toppled
*** Pillar missing

stray a little south of the bearing to find it quickly.

When walking towards the burial ground, somewhere below to the NW is the elusive Kinder Cavern, a cave that no one seems to be able to find. A Ranger informed us he'd been inside it, finding first a shelf and then, further back, a black, bottomless void. Now it's all sealed up, he claimed. The problem is, with the Kinder Cavern, you never know who to believe.

The Kinderlow Bowl Barrow is a typical Bronze Age (2000-1500BC) burial chamber, probably dedicated to a leading family or tribe in the region. The path deviates around it, the fenced area protecting the on-going preservation. One problem had been that walkers had built a cairn from the rocks of the burial ground itself, threatening the site's integrity.

Passing the barrow, continue due west for 350m before descending the steep set of steps off Kinderlow End. At the bottom (SK 06580 86650) there is an intersection of paths, where the route continues west across the fields. The path is well walked, with stiles between the fields, leading steadily downhill for 1km to Tunstead House. There is a distinctive tree that marks the route at that point. Go right (north) around the house, following the drive as it turns back sharply west and joins a metalled road. Finally, follow that road NW for 400m, avoiding the drive to the right, emerging again at the car park.

Route summary

Your present location	Your next objective	Way Point at next objective	Comments
Start at car park at SK 04800 86900	Gate to Water Board access road	SK 05130 87660	900m from the car park, walking NE and north
SK 05130 87660	Set of locked gates. Then take the cobbled path to the left	SK 05280 88000	400m north along access road
SK 05280 88000	Bridge at bottom of William Clough	SK 05930 88740	800m generally NE from the gates
SK 05930 88740	Top of William Clough	SK 06320 90170	1.5km climb, NNE, then turn right (east) on the paving
SK 06320 90170	Top of steep climb up to Kinder SW edge	SK 06800 89700	A stiff 400m climb SE up the steps
SK 06800 89700	Sabre aircraft wreckage above Sandy Heys	SK 07080 89420	Look out for more wreckage to the east of the path
SK 07080 89420	Fence with low stile (having returned to SW edge from wreckage)	SK 07660 89180	The point to make a detour back north to the pillar, about 1km SE
SK 07660 89180	The Edge pillar	SK 07698 89370	300m due north from the path
SK 07698 89370	Back to the stile in the fence on the edge path	SK 07660 89180	300m due south, retracing your steps
SK 07660 89180	Kinder Downfall	SK 08350 88950	800m along the edge
SK 08350 88950	Point above Cluther Rocks	SK 07800 87400	1.5km SSW along the edge from the Downfall
SK 07800 87400	Kinder Low pillar	SK 07904 87059	350m SSE, away from the edge
SK 07904 87059	Kinderlow burial ground	SK 07300 86650	700m SW from the pillar, on a paved path
SK 07300 86650	Bottom of Kinderlow end, where paths cross	SK 06580 86650	800m west, with a steep descent
SK 06580 86650	Tunstead House, with a distinctive tree	SK 05500 86720	1km west, downhill across the fields
SK 05500 86720	Crossroads, go straight across	SK 05200 86760	400m from the house, first N, then WSW
SK 05200 86760	Car park	SK 04800 86900	400m, first NW, then SW

Walk 10 – Edale Moor from Edale village

Start: At the Edale Pay and Display car park – Map reference SK 12430 85320

Distance: 12.8km (8.0 miles)

Total ascent: 500m (1625 ft)

Estimated time: 5 hours

Grading: Moderate

OS map: Explorer map OL 1 The Peak District – Dark Peak area

The route

The route passes through Edale village, rises via The Nab to the Ringing Roger rocks and Nether Tor, before crossing the open moor to the Edale Moor Pillar. From there, it passes two aircraft crash sites and follows the edge of Edale Moor to Crookstone Knoll, before descending into the Edale valley via Crookstone Barn and Clough Farm. The final leg back to the car park is via Roland Cote, Nether Booth and Ollerbrook Booth.

The height profile shows the steep ascent to the pillar and a gently descending homeward leg.

The walk

From the small exit on the western side of the car park, turn right into the road and head north, passing under the railway bridge towards Edale village. Edale is the primary rambling centre for the Kinder Scout area, including the Pennine Way, the longest footpath in England, and the first to be opened (in 1965). Its official start is the Old Nag's Head public house, originally the village smithy. Edale can be reached by train, on the Manchester to Sheffield line, and there is an information centre with an exhibition on local history, as well as providing details of the local geography to help plan your walks.

The road through the village passes a cemetery and a church, eventually running out into a limestone track that reaches a gate to private property (at SK 12200 86120). Take the path through the trees that leads off to the right (NE), descending to a wooden bridge over Grinds Brook and scaling the steps on the opposite embankment into open pastureland.

Follow the paved path north for 200m, turning NE by a stone hut (at SK 12270 86230) along a grassy uphill path towards a wall stile that is just north of an area of woodland. On the other side of the stile, the path veers north again, with a set of stone steps to help the climb, before turning east around the trees. From there, it heads north and then back SE as it zigzags up the incline. At SK 12500 16610,

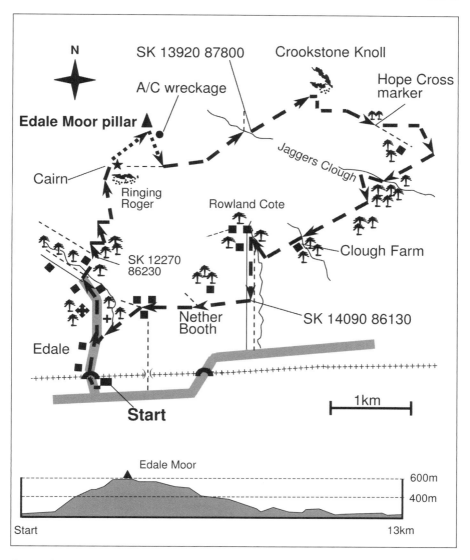

the path turns north yet again, with another path joining the route from Oller Brook to the NE.

As the path climbs northwards, the rocky outcrop of 'Ringing Roger', marking the edge of the Edale moor plateau, is to the fore, the route veering NW and then back NE around the west side of the outcrop. Below the track on the left side is Golden Clough, and looking further back westwards provides a superb view of the Grinds Brook Pennine Way path as it snakes its way towards the heart of the Kinder plateau.

At the top of Golden Clough (SK 12550 87570), our path reaches a cairn marking Nether Tor. From there, the route to the Edale Moor pillar is 450m NENE (compass bearing 059 deg) across peat moor, with numerous water-logged groughs to negotiate. There

Grinds Brook path

may be some faint paths to help you, but as always, such a route is easier in a dry spell or during a hard frost. Coming from the SW, the best approach is to circle round the pillar from the right (east), thereby avoiding a particularly deep water hazard.

The pillar is defended by an expanse of wet peat, with the concrete base being completely exposed by erosion. It is another testimony to the influence of thousands of walkers as they approach the pillar. The top of the pillar is also damaged, with the concrete cracked and the OS insert missing. But the spider remains in place.

The pillar details are:

Position: SK 12927 87809
Flush bracket No: S4231
Height: 590m (1917 ft)
Horizon: 87km (54 miles)
Built: September 1947
Historic use: Secondary
Current use: None
Condition: Poor

From Edale Moor there is line-of-sight to 14 pillars, mostly to the eastern half of the compass. Like the nearby pillar on The Edge (NW

Edale Moor pillar

Pillar	Distance	Direction
Outer Edge	10.3km	NNE (027 deg)
Margery Hill (Primary)	9.8km	ENNE (037 deg)
Back Tor	7.5km	ENE (065 deg)
Rod Moor *	13.3km	E (087 deg)
High Neb	10.1km	EESE (104 deg)
Stanage Edge	13.0km	ESE (111 deg)
Winhill Pike	6.3km	ESE (115 deg)
Sir William Hill	13.1km	SE (139 deg)
Abney Moor	9.8km	ESSE (148 deg)
Bradwell Moor	7.7km	S (178 deg)
Mam Tor	4.2km	S (182 deg)
Kinder Low *	5.0km	WWSW (261 deg)
Higher Shelf Stones	8.0km	WNNW (330 deg)
West End Moor	5.4km	N (359 deg)

* The visibility to Kinder Low and Rod Moor is marginal

Kinder), the views are restricted by the flat ground that surrounds the area, so that the site is not one of the best for appreciating the surrounding geography.

Leaving the pillar on a SESE bearing (120 deg), walk for 150m across the peat and heather towards SK 13040 87750, which marks the small remains of an Avro Hanson aircraft. It crashed during a navigational exercise in December 1944, but all that is left now are small pieces of metal and six memorial crosses to commemorate the dead crew. Turning SSE (151 deg) from there and walking another 100m to SK 13100 87630 brings the route to a second crash site, this one a De Havilland Dragon Rapide aircraft that crashed in December 1963. The wreckage is a little more extensive, with additional debris about 30m away at SK 13070 87620.

From that latter crash site, turn due south. The walking is difficult, across peat bog and heather, but it is only 200m to a path (at around SK 13100 87450) that follows the SW edge of the moor. In fact, there are two such paths, running parallel, about 100m apart. The best one to follow eastwards is the second one to be encountered, closest to the edge (the 'outer' path), that is 300m from the crash site. Both paths are clearly marked on the Explorer OL1 map, but are shown as just one path on some other maps.

Whichever path you find, follow it for 1km, first eastwards, then NE, and finally north until reaching Jaggers Clough. The important waypoint is SK 13920 87800, which is on the outer path where it crosses the clough. If you've followed the inner path, turn right (east) when reaching the clough and walk 100m to the waypoint.

From the clough, continue NE for 500m along the path to a fork at SK 14340 88060. Keep to the right (NE) there, dropping down below Crookstone Knoll. Immediately below the knoll, the route turns SE and descends Crookstone Hill towards a gate at the bottom. The path is easy walking, down a grass track across the moor. Beyond the gate, the track leads towards two trees and a marker post for Hope Cross (at SK 15330 87910), standing alone on the open moorland. Go left (east) at the post. The path going straight ahead is sometimes used by ramblers, and would be a more direct route, but it crosses private land, including a gate with no stile, where no legal right of way has been verified.

From the Hope Cross marker post, the route follows a clear track eastwards to a stile at SK 15830 87850, just a field away from the tree line that marks the SW side of the Ladybower reservoir. Turn right (SE) at the stile, along a rutted track, towards a gate at SK 15990 87610, before turning right again (SW) along another well-worn track, signposted to Edale. This path eventually becomes a crushed limestone track, leading downhill to a wooded area along the lower reaches of Jaggers Clough. Ford the

Roland Cote activity centre

stream there, then follow the track south on the other side, climbing steeply towards Clough Farm.

Following the route around the farm needs a little care. Looking from the apex of the farm drive (where the drive running south is posted as being strictly private), the route proceeds 100m north and then crosses a stream westwards (at SK 14580 86670). Before that, there is another gate and stile on the left. Do not be tempted by that, it leads to a path around the back of the farm, eventually leading down to the road.

Once over the stream, continue west, crossing grass pastures on a well-defined farm track. After 500m, the path veers north along Lady Booth Brook, the Rowland Cote adventure activity centre at Nether Booth coming into view to the west. Run by the Youth Hostel Association, it is one of the best-known locations of its type in the county, offering guidance in climbing, caving and orienteering, as well as accommodation.

Having crossed the Lady Booth Brook, turn south, following the Rowland Cote Centre access drive down to a cattle grid at SK 14090 86130. Passing through the walker's gate on the right, walk west along the grass path to join a short section of farm drive at Nether Booth. Then continue across the field path and on to another farm drive into yet another 'Booth', this one Ollerbrook Booth. In fact, the word originates from 'boothies', which were the shelters used by the shepherds whist they tended their flocks.

Walk westwards through the hamlet, first following the signpost for Edale station, then continuing to a point where the path divides into two, neither of which is signposted. Take the left path (SSW), leading back on to the Edale village road by the cemetery. Turn left there, returning south to the car park.

Route summary

Your present location	Your next objective	Waypoint at next objective	Directions
Start, car park SK 12430 85320	Limestone track, north of village	SK 12200 86120	Walk north through the village, then cross Grinds Brook
SK 12200 86120	Stone hut by paved path	SK 12270 86230	Turn right there, up the grassy slope
SK 12270 86230	At turning north in the rising zigzag path	SK 12500 16610	A path joins from the NE at this point
SK 12500 16610	Cairn at Nether Tor	SK 12550 87570	1km generally north, around 'Ringing Roger'
SK 12550 87570	Edale Moor pillar	SK 12927 87809	450m on an 059 deg bearing from cairn
SK 12927 87809	First aircraft crash site	SK 13040 87750	150m SESE (120 deg) from the pillar
SK 13040 87750	Second aircraft crash site	SK 13100 87630	100m SSE (151 deg) from first crash site
SK 13100 87630	Path following the edge of the moor, one of two running parallel, 100m apart	SK 13100 87450	200m due south across the moor to the first path, another 100m to the second
SK 13100 87450	Ford across Jaggers Clough – **Key Waypoint**	SK 13920 87800	1km east, then NE, along either edge path, and 100m east along the clough if necessary
SK 13920 87800	Fork in path	SK 14340 88060	500m from the clough, go right at the fork
SK 14340 88060	Below Crookstone Knoll, where path turns SE	SK 14700 88260	450m from the fork
SK 14700 88260	Marker post for Hope Cross	SK 15330 87910	800m from the knoll, via a gate. Go left at the post
SK 15330 87910	Stile, leading on to rutted track	SK 15830 87850	500m from the marker post, go right
SK 15830 87850	Rutted track going NE-SW, signposted to Edale, gate to the fore	SK 15990 87610	300m from stile, turn right in front of the gate
SK 15990 87610	Ford across Jaggers Clough	SK 15330 87370	800m SW along the track from the gate
SK 15330 87370	Stream crossing, north of Clough Farm	SK 14580 86670	1.2km SW along the track from Jaggers Clough, and then 100m at the back of the farm
SK 14580 86670	Crossing Lady Booth Brook at Rowland Cote	SK 14040 86600	700m SW, then NW, from Clough Farm
SK 14040 86600	Walker's gate, just after cattle grid	SK 14090 86130	500m south down the Roland Cote drive
SK 14090 86130	Ollerbrook Booth, where path divides	SK 12780 85880	1.3km WSW, take the left of the two paths
SK 12780 85880	Car park	SK 12430 85320	400m on to the Edale village road, then 300m south to car park

Walk 11 – High Neb and Rod Moor

Start: Roadside pull-off on the 'Rod Side' lane that leaves north from the A57 at Hollow Meadows, 3km west of the Rivelin Dams – Map reference SK 25790 88300

Distance: 14km (8.8 miles)

Total ascent: 350m (1137 ft)

Estimated time: 4 hours

Grading: Easy to moderate

OS map: Explorer map OL 1 The Peak District – Dark Peak area

The route

The route uses the lane westwards to Moscar Cross and turns south across the A57 trunk road, then following Stanage Edge to the High Neb pillar and on to Stanedge Pole. The inward leg skirts the Redmires reservoirs, before crossing Hallam Moor to return to the lane. The final section is a short excursion on to the moor, visiting the Rod Moor pillar.

The height profile shows gentle gradients for the majority of the walk, but with a little effort needed out of the Revelin valley at the end of the walk.

The walk

From the parking spot, walk 1.6km west along the lane, passing Crawshaw Head House on the right and then taking the sandstone track westwards as the lane turns sharply south at SK 24190 88400. Pass through two gates, the rutted track joining a better quality drive just before Moscar Cross. The drive then turns SW and, at SK 23170 88310, meets another drive joining from the north.

At the junction stands an ancient signpost, indicating that the location must have been on an old route between Sheffield, Hathersage and Bradfield. It's difficult to say from when the post dates, but its permanent status was utilised by the early surveyors as a location for an arrowhead levelling mark (front base of the pillar). It probably dates back to the First Primary Levelling Initiative carried out by the OS between 1840 and 1860. Like the later, more accurate levelling surveys, where metal flush brackets were used instead of scribed marks, it involved measuring the relative heights between markers (usually about a mile apart). Ultimately, those heights were related to a fixed datum, the Mean Sea Level at Newlyn in Cornwall (for the British mainland).

There are thousands of such marks and flush brackets, but many have been lost to the march of time. They provide yet another objective for the dedicated trigpointer to find and to log.

Continuing the walk, proceed south down the walled drive to the A57 trunk road, passing the impressive Moscar Lodge on the way. Turn right at the road,

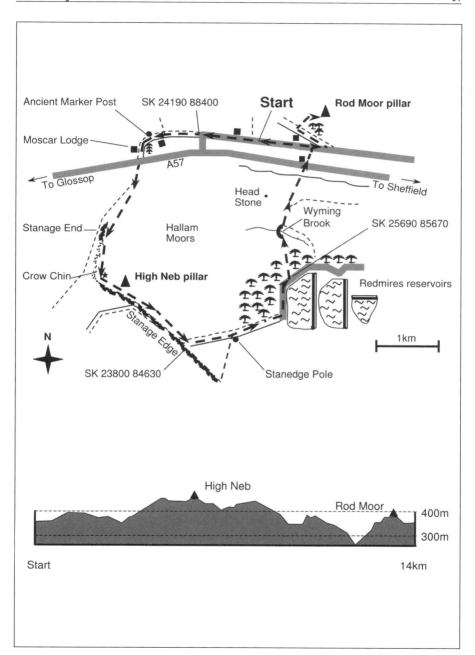

Drinking basin for grouse

crossing to the path marker and stile on the other side. The sandstone path then carries the route south and SSW across the heather moor for 1.5km up to Stanage End. Be wary not to take any paths that leave to the right, they ultimately lead below Stanage Edge. At SK 22640 86720, a narrow path branching to the left provides access to the top, the original path eventually dropping below the edge. Near the top, there is one of several intriguing marker stones inscribed with the letters 'WM'. However, they look too recent to boast any serious historical pedigree, and it may be that 'WM' simply means 'Way Marker'.

The route along the top, south to the cairns at Crow Chin and then turning SW towards the High Neb pillar, is straightforward. The walking is a mixture of gritstone rocks and (usually) wet sand and peat, but with splendid views to the west. On the way, look out for the curious numbered water basins that have been cut into the rocks, each typically 50cm in diameter and a few centimetres deep, with additional catchment grooves. They were cut in the 19th century by gamekeepers to collect rainwater for the grouse, and in dry periods local children were co-opted to keep them full, labouring up and down the edge (perhaps a welcome break from being sent up chimneys with a brush!). There are one hundred in total, numbered so that landowners were not charged more than once for cutting a particular hole.

The High Neb pillar sits on the edge of the Stanage outcrop, with a fine outlook to the west and south, over Bamford and Hathersage. It is in good condition, with the spider, original insert and flush bracket all in place.

The pillar details are:

Position: SK 22816 85344
Flush bracket No: S2157
Height: 458m (1488 ft)
Horizon: 77km (48 miles)
Built: July 1938
Historic use: Secondary
Current use: None
Condition: Good

High Neb pillar

There is line-of-sight to around 16 local pillars, mostly in the western half of the compass. Views NE round to SE are restricted by Hallam Moor and Burbage Moor, so that few of the Sheffield area pillars are in sight. That contrasts with the views from Rod Moor (later in this walk).

From the pillar, continue SW along the edge for 900m, where a dip in the track at SK 23510 84880 allows the first view of the Stanage Causeway running below the edge to the west. It's currently used by four-wheel drive vehicles to reach the top of the edge, but is believed to be part of the 'Long Causeway' Roman road that provided a route across the edge and over the moor for hundreds of years.

Pillar	Distance	Direction
Emlin Ridge *	8.1km	NNNE (008 deg)
Kirk Edge	9.0km	ENNE (033 deg)
Greno Knoll *	14.0km	NE (043 deg)
Rod Moor	4.6km	NE (048 deg)
Ox Stones	5.6km	ESE (114 deg)
Stanage Edge	3.2km	SE (136 deg)
White Edge	10.1km	SSE (159 deg)
Sir William Hill	7.5km	SSSW (190 deg)
Abney Moor *	7.6km	WSSW (219 deg)
Bradwell Moor	11.0km	SWSW (241 deg)
Mam Tor	10.2km	WWSW (260 deg)
Winhill Pike *	4.2km	W (266 deg)
Brown Knoll	14.4km	W (269 deg)
Edale Moor	10.2km	WWNW (284 deg)
West End Moor	12.7km	NWNW (308 deg)
Back Tor	6.4km	WNNW (331 deg)

* The visibility to these pillars is marginal

After a further 900m, the route intercepts the Causeway as it reaches the top of the edge (at SK 23800 84630). Follow the track SE as it veers away from the edge, then walking due east for 700m up to Stanedge Pole, at SK 24690 84430. (Note the different spelling; Stanage Edge vs. Stanedge Pole, but the reason is not understood). The pole is an ancient way-marker, having guided travellers for over four hundred years. The current pole, with its rusting ironwork, is not the original, but the supporting rocks show date carvings as far back as 1550.

From the pole, follow the track NE for 1.2km, descending steadily towards the Redmires reservoirs. On the left is the Redmires Plantation, and on the right is the moorland expanse of Rud Hill and White Stones, an area crossed as part of Walk 14. At the reservoir, turn north, following the perimeter road for 600m past the access drive to Fairthorn Lodge and on to the path marker post at SK 25690 85670 (100m past a car park on the left). Turn north through the gate, following the track to the left of a wall for 150m, through another gate, and finally ascending on to the Open Access area of Hallam Moor.

Initially, the path across the moor follows the left side of a wall, with occasional marshy areas, one crossed by a long boarded pontoon bridge (SK 25640 86030). After 600m, the path negotiates a very wet area (SK 25580 86750), leaving the wall to cross open moorland. The path is clear and well walked, leading after a further 350m to a stone bridge over the Wyming Brook SK 25630 86760. It's an elaborate structure, spanning a drainage channel, part of the water management network for the Redmires reservoirs.

Take the stile by the gate and continue north, ignoring the path that leaves right (east) and the access point to the open moor on the left. On the way across the open moor, the route passes a sturdy evergreen shrub, staking its lone claim in an otherwise bleak landscape of heather and grass. It may be a rhododendron, and it obviously provides some welcome shelter for sheep and other animals under its canopy.

Beyond the shrub, the path continues north, dropping downhill through the heather. At SK 25780 87330, another path crosses the route from the west, coming from the distinctive 'Head Stone' and continuing to the east. Ignore it, and follow the route markers north down a path to a wooden bridge at SK 25790 87650. (Much of the time, that path is also a small stream). Cross the river on the bridge and climb the other side, following the path over two stiles and eventually reaching the A57 trunk road at Hollow Meadow (SK 25890 87750).

Cross the road and turn right for 20m, taking the wall stile that accesses pastureland to the NE. The route then continues NE over two more stiles, before turning due north and rising steeply up to the lane below Rod Moor. Turn right (east) there, even though the car will be in view some 300m to the west, and walk 130m to the bottom of Crawshaw Lodge Drive. Follow the drive WNW up to a gate and stile, passing the lodge on the way. Usually, there will be some 20 peacocks and peahens displaying their plumage, either in the lodge gardens or flying across to the moor to roost in the trees.

At the stile, take the narrow sheep path that runs back diagonally NE up the hill to the right, through the heather towards the top of the small wooded area (which is strictly private). There, at SK 26170 88430, the wall has fallen, repaired with a makeshift stone stile and a single strand of wire, so that it is easy to step over. It is open land on both sides of the wall, so there are no issues of access, but as always, take care not to disturb any more stones from the wall. From there, the pillar is visible 100m east across the grass moor.

The pillar details are:

Position: SK 26268 88413
Flush bracket No: S2299
Height: 384m (1248 ft)
Horizon: 70km (44 miles)
Built: October 1938
Historic use: Secondary
Current use: None
Condition: Good

Rod Moor pillar

Rod Moor trig point is an un-distinguished site, but the pillar is sound, with all its original features, even if it does look somewhat unkempt. It has line-of-sight to at least 17 local pillar sites, but many of them are in the Sheffield urban area, and five of those are missing. The best views are from SE round to SW, including the areas of Stanage Edge and Hallam Moor visited by this walk.

From the pillar, retrace your steps over the wall and down to the gate, perhaps again pausing to admire the colourful birds at Crawshaw Lodge. From there it's down to the lane, turning right at the bottom and walking back to the start along the lane.

Pillar	Distance	Direction
Kirk Edge	4.7km	NNE (017 deg)
Greno Knoll	9.4km	NE (040 deg)
Loxley Common	5.3km	ENE (064 deg)
Hill Top (Sheffield)	14.1km	ENE (071 deg)
Wincobank Hill **	11.8km	EENE (077 deg)
Shirecliffe Gunsite **	8.8km	EENE (082 deg)
The Herdings **	12.4km	ESE (116 deg)
Meadow Head **	10.1km	SESE (128 deg)
Coal Aston **	13.7km	SE (131 deg)
Ringinglow	6.0km	ESSE (142 deg)
Ox Stones	5.6km	SSE (162 deg)
Stanage Edge	5.5km	SSSW (192 deg)
High Neb	4.50km	SW (228 deg)
Edale Moor	13.3km	W (267 deg)
Back Tor	7.0km	WNW (291 deg)
Emlin Ridge	5.4km	NNW (335 deg)
Whitwell Moor *	8.9km	NNNW (351 deg)

* The visibility to Whitwell Moor is marginal
** Pillar missing

Route summary

Your present location	Your next objective	Waypoint at next objective	Directions
Start, roadside pull-off SK 25790 88300	Track leaving west at bend in lane	SK 24190 88400	1.6km west along the lane
SK 24190 88400	Ancient signpost	SK 23170 88310	1.1km west and SW, past Moscar Cross
SK 23170 88310	A57 trunk road, to stile on south side	SK 23130 87890	400m south from post, go right for 20m at road
SK 23130 87890	Narrow path to left, accessing Stanage End,	SK 22640 86720	900m SSE along moor path
SK 22640 86720	High Neb pillar	SK 22816 85344	1.5km south and SW along the Edge
SK 22816 85344	Causeway, joining from below	SK 23800 84630	1.5km SE along the Edge
SK 23800 84630	Stanedge Pole	SK 24690 84430	500m SE and east along Causeway
SK 24690 84430	Path marker post and gate	SK 25690 85670	1.8km, first NE by the plantation, then north alongside reservoir
SK 25690 85670	Boarded pontoon bridge	SK 25640 86030	400m north, moor path follows wall
SK 25640 86030	Stone bridge over dyke	SK 25630 86760	700m north on moor path
SK 25630 86760	Path crosses route, from Head Stone (to west)	SK 25780 87330	500m NNE along moor path
SK 25780 87330	A57 trunk road. Go right for 20m at road, to stile	SK 25890 87750	500m north and then NE, over stream.
SK 25890 87750	Lane below Rod Moor (car visible 300m west)	SK 26050 88260	600m NE and north, over two stiles
SK 26050 88260	Crawshaw Lodge Drive	SK 26210 88270	130m east along the lane
SK 26210 88270	Gate and stile	SK 26050 88350	200m WNW up the drive
SK 26050 88350	Access point over fallen wall	SK 26170 88430	150m NE along sheep path, to corner of plantation
SK 26170 88430	Rod Moor pillar	SK 26268 88413	100m east across moor from fallen wall
SK 26268 88413	Crawshaw Lodge Drive	SK 26210 88270	Retrace the route back to the lane
SK 26210 88270	Starting point on roadside pull-off	SK 25790 88300	300m west along the lane

Walk 12 – Mam Tor and Brown Knoll

Start: At the Mam Nick car park off the A625, just east of the turning for Edale. Map Reference SK 12400 83200

Distance: 15km (9.4 miles)

Total ascent: 530m (1720 ft)

Estimated time: 5 hours

Grading: Moderate

OS map: Explorer map OL 1 The Peak District – Dark Peak area

The Route

The route leads to the summit of Mam Tor, then down across the Edale valley, before passing through Barber Booth and ascending 'Jacob's Ladder' to the SW edge of Kinder Scout. From there it returns via the Brown Knoll pillar, across the moor and along Rushup Edge back to the start.

The gradient profile shows the initial steep ascent to Mam Tor summit, then a period of easy walking before the long climb up to the edge of Kinder, followed by a gentle descent to end the walk.

The walk

Leave the car park in a northerly direction, via a flight of stone steps, turning east at the top and emerging on to the Edale lane. Pass through the stile-gate on the corner of the road, taking the well-made stone path up to the Mam Tor summit and pillar. At the top, there are superb views of the Edale, Hope and Castleton valleys. If the weather is clear, you'll be able see the Grindsbrook skyline of the Kinder plateau to the NW, Rushup Edge (from where the route returns) to the west, Shining Tor to the SW and the scarred hillside quarry at Small Dale to the south. There are also excellent views along the Great Ridge to Winhill Pike and Stanage Edge to the NE and east.

Mam Tor is a typical Bronze Age hill fort, dating back some 3000 years. The old ramparts to the north and the west, which in their day would have been defended by a wooden palisade, are still clearly visible. The round hut dwellings, where the beleaguered inhabitants could retreat in safety from other marauding tribes, were all positioned between the ramparts and the summit, along with their stores and livestock. You'll appreciate the best views of the site when returning along Rushup Edge at the end of the walk.

Looking from the SE of the summit, there is a good view of Castleton. But caution is needed; Mam Tor is a constantly moving mountain, scarred by a major slippage on the SE face. Far below, the old road into Castleton has been severed, and is no longer passable to traffic. Also visible below is the Blue John cavern,

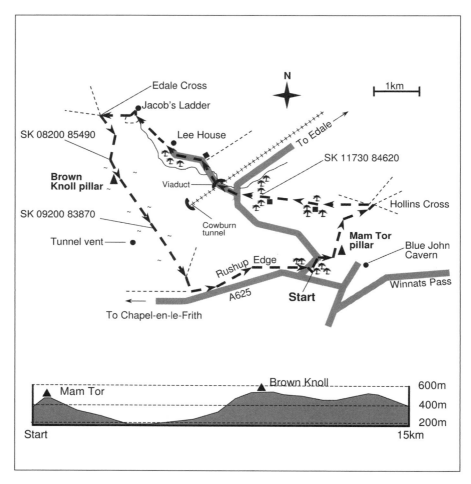

where the attractive, semi-precious Blue John mineral was mined for its orna-
mental and jewellery value. As well as the Blue John cave, with guided tours to
the depths of the cavern, there is the Speedwell mine at the bottom of Winnat's
Pass, where the visit takes place in a boat, negotiating a labyrinth of underground
tunnels. Winnat's Pass itself is spectacular, the deep gorge having been cut by a
torrent of raging water as the last glaciers retreated at the end of the Ice Age.

The triangulation pillar on the summit of Mam Tor is unusual in that it is
made from local stone, cemented to form a pyramid shape. Hotine did permit
this, provided that the resultant pillar met his standards for precision and
strength. It remains in reasonable condition, but the original OS insert in the spider has been lost, being replaced by a plastic plug.

The pillar details are:

Position: SK 12769 83612
Flush bracket No: S4230
Height: 517m (1680 ft)
Horizon: 81km (51 miles)
Built: September 1947
Historic use: Secondary
Current use: None
Condition: Fair

From Mam Tor there is line-of-sight to at least 13 other pillars, with views all round the compass. Technically, there are several more, for instance to Shining Tor near Buxton, but the long distances means there is little chance of picking out the pillars.

From the Mam Tor pillar, follow the paved path along the 'Great Ridge' for 1.5km, descending to the Hollins Cross saddle at SK 13580 84510, with its distinctive memorial. Take the path that leaves from the north side of the ridge, back in a westerly direction towards 'Greenlands',

Mam Tor pillar

Pillar	Distance	Direction
Edale Moor	4.2km	N (002 deg)
Margery Hill (Primary)	13.6km	NNE (027 deg)
Back Tor	10.2km	NE (044 deg)
Winhill Pike	6.1km	EENE (076 deg)
High Neb	10.2km	EENE (080 deg)
Stanage Edge	12.3km	E (093 deg)
Abney Moor	15.1km	SSE (160 deg)
Bradwell Moor	3.5km	SSSE (173 deg)
Bee Low *	5.7km	WSSW (218 deg)
Black Edge	9.3km	SW (225 deg)
Ladder Hill	11.1km	WSW (245 deg)
Brown Knoll	4.7km	WNW (289 deg)
Kinder Low	6.0km	NWNW (306 deg)

* Pillar missing

setting your objective as SK 12560 84470. Avoid the path from Hollins Cross that goes due north, as this leads to Nether Booth. Likewise, as you walk westwards towards Greenlands, steer clear of a second path that leaves to the right, that one leading NW to Edale village.

The path to Greenlands is straightforward, emerging over a stile on to a rough drive, 1km from Hollins Cross. Turn right at that point, following the direction post to Edale. The drive quickly becomes a metalled road, twisting below a tree-lined canopy; it's a surprising contrast to the rest of the walk. 300m along the lane, after turning a sharp right-hand bend, look for a stile at the top of the embankment on the left (west) at SK 12390 84600. It leads to a path across open fields. Beware, it's easy to make a mistake here and find yourself on a path that goes back south through the wooded area.

The path across the fields is a little obscure. Keep on a westerly bearing, heading for SK 11730 84620, which is the stile marking the path through the wooded area. The official path passes just to the north of a stone building, but it's easy to stray too far north, missing the access point through the wood. From the other side of the wood, the path reaches the Edale lane just opposite the road to Barber Booth, which is the direction the route will follow. It's pleasant walking, first passing under the Edale to Chinley railway arches (some welcome shelter for a refreshment break in poor weather), then on to Upper Booth (1km distant). There, the route joins the Pennine Way, near its most southerly starting point. It's a famous path that many walkers aspire to complete, stretching over 400km (250 miles) to the Scottish border, and passing by or near to some 40 or more OS pillars.

500m beyond Upper Booth is Lee House information centre, often a hive of activity, the owners making rural furniture from reclaimed wood and rearing rare animal breeds. After that, the track leads on for another 1km to the bridge at the bottom of 'Jacob's Ladder', a steep flight of stone steps taking the route up towards the Kinder plateau. The name is not biblically derived; it originates from the man who built it, Jacob Marshall of Edale Head Farm. But it's a common name for stone staircases; for instance, there is another at Dove Dale in the south of the Peak District.

The bridge, with the plaque describing Jacob's Ladder nearby, is an alternative refreshment point before making the steep climb. There is a choice of the steps or the more gradual ascent up the cobbled donkey track that loops round to the west, the old route taken historically by the salt ponies. Both paths arrive at the same place near the top, with the Pym Chair and Crowden Tower rocks visible on the Kinder skyline as you walk up.

The top is marked by a gate at Edale Cross (SK 08090 86090). There, the Pennine Way continues north, whilst our route turns south along a paved path towards Brown Knoll. After 700m, cross the fence over a stile on the left (SK 08200 85490) and continue SSE (bearing 158 deg). In poor weather, it will be helpful to use your GPS to home in on the pillar (at SK 08369 85129), the area being wet peat bog with no single established path. It is 400m to the pillar from the fence crossing point.

A few years ago, the Brown Knoll Pillar was pushed over by vandals. But it has been successfully righted, with a new reinforced plinth, so that it can be classed as being undisturbed, exactly on its original spot. It's in good structural condition, but has a replacement resin plug in the spider.

The pillar details are:

Position: SK 08369 85129
Flush bracket No: S2782
Height: 560m (1820 ft)
Horizon: 85km (53 miles)
Built: April 1940
Historic use: Secondary
Current use: None
Condition: Good

Brown Knoll pillar

It has line-of-sight to some of the peaks that were visible from Mam Tor, but with wider views westwards and with some of the views north and NE blocked by the Kinder plateau. For instance, the Edale Moor pillar is not quite visible.

From the pillar, the route heads SE, with over 2km of featureless moor to negotiate. Use a waypoint at SK 09200 83870 as a position to aim for; it's the point where the route crosses over the Cowburn railway tunnel, identified by a castellated air vent 300m to the WSW. There is a path of sorts, but it's often prudent to find your own route around the deepest waterlogged gullies. The next waypoint is at

Pillar	Distance	Direction
Rod Moor	18.2km	EENE (080 deg)
High Neb	14.4km	E (089 deg)
Winhill Pike	10.3km	E (090 deg)
Stanage Edge	16.7km	E (094 deg)
Mam Tor	4.7km	ESE (109 deg)
Bradwell Moor	6.9km	SE (136 deg)
Wormhill	9.8km	SSSE (166 deg)
Bee Low *	5.1km	SSSE (172 deg)
Fairfield	10.7km	S (183 deg)
Black Edge	8.4km	SSSW (195 deg)
Ladder Hill	8.4km	SW (222 deg)
Chinley Churn	5.0km	WSW (253 deg)
Lantern Pike *	5.6km	WNW (295 deg)
Kinder Low	2.0km	NNNW (347 deg)

* Pillar missing or toppled

SK 09840 83160, where a path from Barber Booth joins from the NE. The route continues south for 250m from there, meeting the path that turns east along Rushup Edge (at SK 09920 82900).

The homeward leg back to the start is 3km of straightforward walking along Rushup Edge, following a stone wall. The final stages provide splendid views into Edale on the north side and the growing vista of Mam Tor to the fore, the ramparts and the geography of the hill fort being clearly visible. If you're lucky, you'll be entertained by dozens of paragliders who turn out at all times of the year to take advantage of the rising air currents generated by the ridge.

But before leaving the end of the ridge, ready to regain the car park, take a long look at the Edale valley. It has the classic appearance of a glacial valley, with its broad 'U' shape. Around one hundred thousand years ago, the unremitting snows would have built a huge mass of ice at the head, below the Brown Knoll moor, the weight then pushing slowly down the valley towards Hope, relentlessly cutting through the landscape. Compared to the similar examples in Wales (e.g. the Snowdon Horseshoe, Cader Idris and Cader Berwyn) or the Lake District (Helvellyn), it's a very modest illustration. But it's sobering to think that such conditions may one day return, despite our present spell of global warming.

Route summary

Your present location	Your next objective	Waypoint at next objective	Directions
Start, Mam Nick SK 12400 83200	Stile gate on Edale road	SK 12500 83430	From the car, N up the steps and to the road
SK 12500 83430	Mam Tor pillar	SK 12769 83612	Up the steps to the top
SK 12769 83612	Hollins Cross	SK 13580 84510	Walk 1.5km NE along the ridge from the pillar
SK 13580 84510	Lane at 'Greenlands'	SK 12560 84470	1km westwards. At the lane, turn right (north)
SK 12560 84470	Field stile leading to path west	SK 12390 84600	300m down the lane, just after the covered lane turns sharp right
SK 12390 84600	Stile to path through the wood	SK 11730 84620	Path passes just north of a stone building
SK 11730 84620	Edale lane	SK 11330 84660	Take the lane opposite, to Barber Booth
SK 11330 84660	Lee House	SK 09660 85510	Follow the lane for 2km from the Edale lane
SK 09660 85510	Bridge at bottom of Jacob's Ladder	SK 08820 86140	Follow the track for 1km from Lee House
SK 08820 86140	Edale Cross, top of Jacob's Ladder	SK 08090 86090	A steep climb up the steps from the bridge
SK 08090 86090	Fence stile	SK 08200 85490	800m south. Paved path for much of the way to the stile
SK 08200 85490	Brown Knoll pillar	SK 08369 85129	400m SE across peat bog (bearing 158 deg)
SK 08369 85129	Point above the railway tunnel, with the vent to the WSW	SK 09200 83870	It's 1.5km SE across the peat moor
SK 09200 83870	Barber Booth path joins from the NE, after 1km SE across the peat moor	SK 09840 83160	Carry on south at that point
SK 09840 83160	Rushup Edge path.	SK 09920 82900	A further 250m SE. There, turn right (east) along the Edge
SK 09920 82900	Car park	SK 12400 83200	3km NE and E along Rushup Edge back to Edale lane and the Mam Nick car park

Walk 13 – Win Hill Pike from Hope

Start: In the centre of Hope – Map Reference SK 17190 83500

Distance: 12km (7.5 miles)

Total ascent: 520m (1,690 ft)

Estimated time: 4 hours

Grading: Moderate

OS map: Explorer map OL 1 The Peak District – Dark Peak area

The route

The route begins across open pastures around Lose Hill, before crossing the lane at Edale End and climbing past Wooler Knoll and Thornhill Brink on the way to the Win Hill summit. Return is via Aston and back into Hope.

The height profile shows a modest start, a respite, then a steep climb and descent over Win Hill.

The walk

Walk north out of Hope along Edale Road, taking a path through the wall on the west side at SK 17160 83890. It's directly opposite the lane that leads to the cemetery. After passing several buildings and enclosures, the path emerges into grass pastures, turning NW along a well-trodden route that runs 2km across pleasant countryside, towards Losehill Farm. Just before reaching the farm, the route turns NE (at SK 15910 84690) along a well-defined farm track, with good views back towards the Hope valley, Castleton and the bottom of Winnat's Pass.

Hope is currently a modest, but thriving Peak District tourism centre, and in

Lose Hill from the east

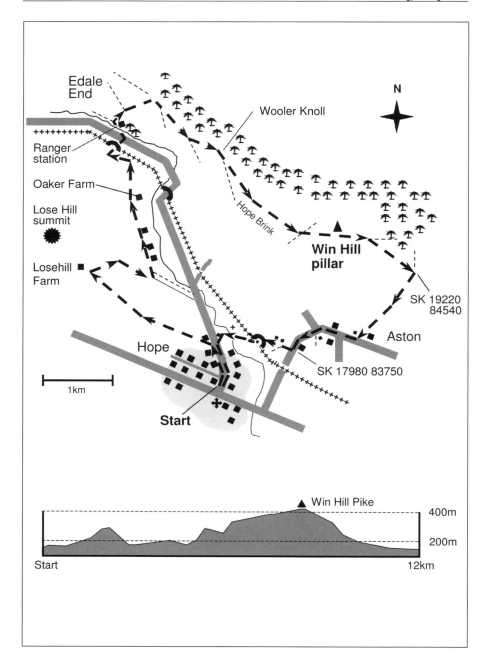

Edale End

Wooler Knoll

N

Ranger station

Oaker Farm

Lose Hill summit

Hope Brink

Losehill Farm

Win Hill pillar

SK 19220 84540

Aston

1km

Hope

SK 17980 83750

Start

Win Hill Pike

400m

200m

Start   12km

Bronze Age times it occupied a similar centre of activity. It was at the very heart of the primary mule paths that were used to transport essential materials like salt, wine and spices, continuing in that role for hundreds of years, up to and beyond the Roman occupation.

It is only when walking away from Losehill Farm that the view of the Lose Hill summit can be fully appreciated. It will dominate the skyline on your west side for the next 2km, as the route drops down south-eastwards to the metalled track at Townshead (SK 16560 84630), before turning north towards Oaker Farm. As the path descends, on the other side of the valley to your front there is a good view of the tree-lined edge at Wooler Knoll, the route that will eventually lead towards the pillar at Win Hill.

A most interesting story about these two hills is the legend of the great battle of AD626 between arch-rivals King Edwin of Northumberland and King Cuicholm of Wessex. It was Cuicholm who boasted by far the bigger army, and he swept down confidently from his camp on Lose Hill, forcing his opponent Edwin back to his fortifications on Win Hill. But, when you reach that summit, you'll appreciate how the tables were turned, the attacking army struggling up the rough terrain only to perish to a man under a hail of rocks and boulders. So that possibly explains the names of the two hills, but it is only a legend!

Keeping the loser's camp to the west, the track passes Oaker Farm, where the owners have constructed an easy detour to avoid intrusion. And it's in such an area that you might be lucky enough to stumble upon a rural craft like dry-stone walling. Such is the love that some people have for conservation, they will pay to be allowed to undertake such wall construction!

After the farm, the path enters a wide meadow, prior to descending towards a

Dry-stone walling; a skilled craft

short drive at Edale End. Turn right on that drive, pass under the railway bridge (at SK 16070 86220), cross the road and walk SE for some 50m, entering the wooded area to the east via a stile. Exit the other side of the trees, following the track north past the Ranger Station. Then, at the top of the drive, turn east around the back of the building. There, look for a signpost marked 'Hope Cross' (SK 16100 86430) on the gate and take the path that heads NE alongside the wall. That path rises quickly across the lower meadows, the route heading for the stile in the top right-hand corner, after which it follows the wall NE up the steep fern-clad slope.

As the path reaches higher ground, the view behind expands to reveal the entire Edale valley, with its characteristic glacial 'U' shape. To the NW is the Kinder Scout plateau and Brown Knoll. On the south side of the valley, Lose Hill and the Great Ridge lead westwards to Mam Tor, and to the more distant south is Abney Moor.

At map reference SK16320 86730, cross the stile and head NE for 200m, joining the old Roman Road that runs SE along Wooler Knoll. At SK16890 86240, take the path ESE, leaving the Roman Road as it veers away to the right, then turn SE to walk along the Hope Brink ridge. The walking is excellent, with Win Hill pike coming into view as the path reaches Thornhill Brink (1.2km from Wooler Knoll), before it turns east towards the pillar (1km distant). Approaching the summit, the Ladybower reservoir and the arched bridge carrying the A57 trunk road come into view below, to the NE.

As the distinct 'pike' on Win Hill becomes more evident, with its rugged outline set against the sky, it's easy to see how King Edwin might have prevailed over an army trying to take his position. That's assuming, of course, that the legend has any truth!

The triangulation pillar is in good condition, with its original spider and plug intact. Its base is exposed, but remains solid. It's a very popular spot, so that the local sheep have become accustomed to walkers. Be prepared to share your sandwiches!

The pillar details are:

Position: SK 18678 85093
Flush bracket No: S4228
Height: 463m (1,505 ft)
Horizon: 77km (48 miles)
Built: September 1947
Historic use: Secondary
Current use: None
Condition: Good

Win Hill pillar

The pillar triangulates with at least 16 others, a surprising number considering it's not the highest vantage point in the area. Its position on the very pronounced peak allows particularly good views up the Derwent valley towards peaks that can't easily be seen from Mam Tor, the higher pillar at the western end of the Great Ridge.

Pillar	Distance	Direction
Margery Hill (Primary)	10.6km	N (001 deg)
Back Tor	6.0km	NNNE (011 deg)
Kirk Edge	11.9km	NE (049 deg)
High Neb	4.1km	EESE (097 deg)
Stanage Edge	6.7km	ESE (108 deg)
Flask Edge	11.6km	SESE (123 deg)
White Edge	12.0km	SE (140 deg)
Sir William Hill	7.8km	SSE (159 deg)
Abney Moor	5.7km	SSSW (187 deg)
Bradwell Moor	7.4km	SW (228 deg)
Mam Tor	6.1km	WWSW (256 deg)
Brown Knoll	10.3km	W (270 deg)
Kinder Low	10.9km	WWNW (281 deg)
Edale Moor	6.4km	WNW (296 deg)
Higher Shelf Stones	13.8km	NW (315 deg)
Outer Edge	11.9km	N (356 deg)

From the pillar, walk east towards the forest, down the steep track. It's littered with loose stones, and can be particularly slippery in wet conditions. At the stile gate, veer right (SE), away from the path that goes on towards the trees, following the track downwards until meeting an adjoining path coming in from the left (at SK 19220 84540). Turn right there, following the path round to the SW, finally dropping down into a field. The next stile is in the bottom right-hand corner of that field, leading on to a pleasant grassy meadow enclosed by walls and trees, the path finally emerging at the bottom on to Thornhill Lane in Aston (SK 18680 83930). Turn right (west) there. It's very pleasant walking, but somewhat claustrophobic, some areas being enveloped in a low canopy of trees and bounded by steep banks with dark, sinister root formations.

Walk 1km westwards along the lane to SK 17980 83750, turning right into a drive indicated as leading to the cemetery. After 150m, the drive reaches a fork; keep left, the drive then passing under a railway bridge before reaching the cemetery itself and coming to a T-junction. Turn left over a small river bridge and walk 100m up the hill, back to the start of the walk on Edale Road.

Route summary

Your present location	Your next objective	Waypoint at next objective	Directions
Start in centre of Hope SK 17190 83500	Stile on west side of Edale Road, opposite lane to cemetery	SK 17160 83890	400m north along the road
SK 17160 83890	Where a path leaves to the SW to Spring House Farm	SK 16400 84190	100m west from the road, then 800m NW
SK 16400 84190	Losehill Farm	SK 15910 84690	A further 700m NW
SK 15910 84690	Metalled road at Townsend	SK 16560 84630	800m, generally east, following the track
SK 16560 84630	Railway bridge at Edale End	SK 16070 86220	2km north, past Oaker Farm, joining a track to the road
SK 16070 86220	Gate on north side of Ranger Station, with sign to Hope Cross	SK 16100 86430	Cross the road, through the wood, up the drive and round the Station
SK 16100 86430	Wall stile	SK 16320 86730	400m NE along the wall
SK 16320 86730	Wooler Knoll	SK 16890 86240	200m east to the Roman road, then 600m SSE
SK 16890 86240	Thornhill Brink	SK 17920 84970	1.8km along Hope Brink
SK 17920 84970	Win Hill pillar	SK 18678 85093	800m due east
SK 18678 85093	Path joins from the NE	SK 19220 84540	Total 750m, first east, then SSE, over a stile, then SE
SK 19220 84540	Down to the lane in Aston	SK 18680 83930	800m SW, following the path
SK 18680 83930	Right turning to the cemetery	SK 17980 83750	900m along the lane through Aston
SK 17980 83750	Lane forking off to the right	SK 17840 83830	150m, keep straight on, don't go right
SK 17840 83830	Near the cemetery	SK 17230 84000	700m along the lane, under the railway bridge
SK 17230 84000	Hope centre	SK 17190 83500	Turn left, up the hill to Edale Road, then left into town

Walk 14 – Ox Stones and Stanage Edge

Start: Lay-by on lane ('School Lane'), 3.5km after leaving the A6187 to the NE from Hathersage – Map Reference SK 25330 82580

Distance: 13.5km (8.5 miles)

Total ascent: 400m (1300 ft)

Estimated time: 4 hours

Grading: Easy to moderate

OS map: Explorer map OL 1 The Peak District – Dark Peak area

The route

From School Lane, the route crosses Higger Tor and the Carl Walk hill fort to the south, before turning east over Burbage Edge and Burbage Moor to reach the Ox Stones pillar. From there, it goes north and west across Rud Hill and White Stones, returning via Stanedge Pole, Stanage Edge and the Stanage Edge pillar.

The height profile shows relatively gentle gradients for the majority of the walk, but with a little effort needed when walking up from Burbage Clough, and again from the reservoir to Stanedge Pole.

The walk

Exit the lay-by over the fence stile to the south of the lane, selecting the path that runs SE. (Two other paths leave south and SW, towards Callow Bank). Follow the path for 400m across moorland grass to a stile preceding a lane at SK 25630 82290, crossing to the stile opposite and taking the path that rises towards the top of Higger Tor. It's a rocky plateau, with outcrops to the south and east, providing some challenges for rock climbers

From the top, the view to the SE includes the Iron Age hill fort of Carl Wark, the next objective on the walk. There are a number of ways to exit the top of Higger Tor to the south, but the easiest is probably at SK 25650 81940, dropping down a rocky descent to a path leading directly to the NW corner of the hill fort. Carl Wark dates from around 500BC, so it's younger than the fort visited at Mam Tor during Walk 12, and it may have been used well into the period of Roman occupation, up to 400AD.

At the NW approach, to the right of the path there is an information plaque. It gives a brief insight into the history of hill forts and their role as settlements, defended against marauding tribes. On top, the plateau is strewn with rocks, and there is evidence of extra stonewall defences erected by the various occupants. To live there, and to defend it, could hardly have been a comfortable existence.

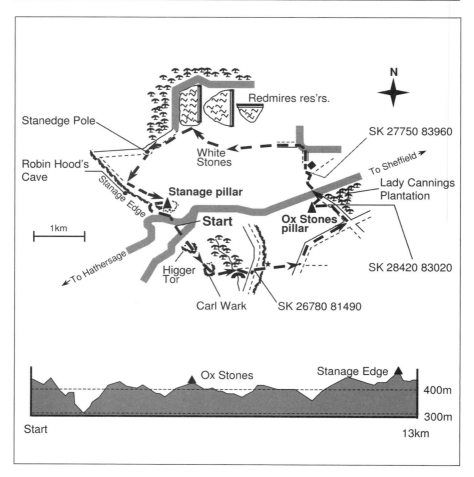

The path off the hill fort is at the eastern end, at SK 26020 81430. Follow it down, heading due east to the southern tip of an area of woodland and crossing the packhorse bridge over Burbage Clough. From the other side, turn SE, climbing away from the wood for 250m, there meeting a track crossing SW-NE (at SK 26580 81270). Turn left on to the track (NE), walking for 300m below the rocky outcrops of Burbage Edge, up to a marker post at SK 26780 81490. Taking the marked path that runs east, cut through a natural break in the line of Burbage Edge, continuing for 280m to a point where a path along the top of the Edge crosses the route. It's marked by two cairns, at SK 27060 81520. Keep straight on (ENE), following the clearly defined gritstone and peat path across the expanse of Burbage Moor, with the Ox Stones pillar just visible (weather permitting) on the skyline, about 1.8km to the NNE.

Ox Stones rock formations

At SK 27660 81660, 600m on from Burbage Edge, the route reaches the Houndkirk Road, a rutted sandstone track that can accommodate four-wheel drive vehicles, but one that is also used by the scrambler bike enthusiasts. Turn left on to the road, following it for 1.4km, first NNE, and then NE, reaching a path crossing right to left at SK 28610 82640. Turn left (NW), following the track up to the SW edge of the Lady Canning's Plantation, there locating a faint path through the heather on the left, some 450m after leaving the Houndkirk Road. It leaves the main path at SK 28420 83020 leading, after 300m, to the Ox Stones pillar and the Ox Stones rock formations.

The pillar is in good condition, with the spider, OS plug and flush bracket all intact, whilst the Ox Stones them-selves sit some 100m to the west. Like the formations seen on Derwent Edge (Walk 8), the gritstone rocks have been left standing whilst all around has been eroded by the elements.

The pillar details are:

Position: SK 28021 83134
Flush bracket No: S2159
Height: 420m (1365 ft)
Horizon: 73km (46 miles)
Built: July 1938
Historic use: Secondary
Current use: None
Condition: Good

Ox Stones pillar

There is line-of-sight to around 16 local pillars, including a group towards the NE in the Sheffield area. Pillars to the SE are obscured by the Burbage and Houndkirk moors, whilst Ringinglow, only 2km to the east, is blocked by Lady Canning's Plantation. Burbage Edge cuts off some views to the SW and west, but visibility to the pillars in the NW and north is good, with Kirk Edge just in sight over the top of the plantation.

Pillar	Distance	Direction
Greno Knoll	13.2km	NNE (019 deg)
Loxley Common	8.2km	NNE (021 deg)
Top End	11.6km	NNE (024 deg)
Birley Edge	11.2km	ENNE (029 deg)
Shirecliffe Gunsite *	9.5km	NE (047 deg)
Wincobank Hill *	12.5km	NENE (051 deg)
Grange Hill	10.1km	SSE (160 deg)
Flask Edge	4.3km	SSSE (173 deg)
Stanage Edge	2.9km	W (268 deg)
High Neb	5.7km	WNW (293 deg)
Back Tor	11.4km	NW (314 deg)
Margery Hill (Primary)	15.5km	WNNW (324 deg)
Emlin Ridge	11.0km	NNW (338 deg)
Rod Moor	5.6km	NNW (341 deg)
Whitwell Moor	14.4km	NNNW (348 deg)
Kirk Edge	9.8km	N (358 deg)

* Pillar missing

From the pillar, walk across to the Ox Stones rocks, there identifying the path that begins from SK 27940 83160, leading first north, then NW through the heather, down to a gate at the west-facing corner of the plantation. It's often waterlogged, but clearly well walked. After the gate (SK 27850 83430), exit on to the lane and turn right for 15m, taking the stile on the north side, then following the path northwards across the grass moor.

After 400m, the route reaches a marker post at SK 27830 83870, with three paths leaving to the fore. Take the right hand path, bearing NE, following it for 100m to a point at SK 27910 83910. Turn WNW there, continuing for 180m across a grass field to a stile in the corner, at SK 27750 83960. That accesses a farm track, flanked by stone walls, leading through Brown Edge Farm, then northwards, exiting on to a lane (Fullwood Road) at the end of the farm drive (SK 27820 84560).

Turn left on the lane, walking 120m to a right-hand bend, there taking the ladder stile over the wall on the left, accessing a fenced and walled track. Follow the track due west for 250m to a double gate, where the route then follows the right side of a wall, passing a small, closed reservoir. After a further 250m, the path reaches a second ladder stile, at SK 27220 84580, taking the route on to the moorland area of Rud Hill.

The path across the moor runs west for 1.5km, with a series of regular marker posts and stiles to guide the way, the latter section having the Redmires reservoir in view to the north. The ground can be very wet, so that numerous excursions left and right are needed to follow the path around the more boggy areas, but the route is clear and well walked.

At SK 25850 84580 (Key waypoint), near White Stones, the path veers abruptly NNW for 400m, descending towards the SW corner of the reservoirs and crossing some very wet ground. At SK 25770 84960, the path turns west

Not Robin Hood's cave!

again, crossing two brooks some 50m apart. After the second brook, take the right of the two paths to the fore, walking 50m steeply uphill (WNW) to a stone pillar at the corner of a fenced area. Skirt round the top of the fenced area, walking north for 50m to a ladder stile (SK 25610 85020), then turn left, following the peat path alongside the fence. It runs SW for 800m towards Stanedge Pole, steadily converging with the sandstone track that skirts the Redmires Plantation, the same track that formed part of the route used during Walk 11 to High Neb and Rod Moor.

At Stanedge Pole (SK 24680 84420), take the path that leaves SW through the heather and across wet grass moorland. As usual, several detours may be needed to negotiate the waterlogged area, the path eventually reaching Stanage Edge at around SK 24380 83770. The route now turns SE, keeping to the top of the Edge, such that it's not easy to appreciate the dramatic gritstone outcrops. The Edge is best viewed from below, where the rock climbers have a multitude of difficult routes to attempt, making it one of the most popular climbing venues in the Peak District.

200m SE along the Edge is the so-called 'Robin Hood's Cave' (SK 24440 83580), abounding with legends. In fact, looking back north from the access point, the rock-strewn overhang is not the cave at all. The actual cave is 20m further north, out of view, and is accessible only by climbing up from the bottom. Whether Robin Hood himself used it as a refuge is unknown, but in recent history it has provided a night camp for climbers, vagrants and teenage parties alike.

From the area of the cave, continue SE along the Edge for 1km, picking a route amongst the boulders, up to the Stanage Edge Pillar. It's firmly planted on its rock base, immune from erosion, so that it remains in excellent condition. But the OS insert has been lost, replaced by a plastic plug.

The pillar details are:

Position: SK 25094 83017
Flush bracket No: S2156
Height: 457m (1485 ft)
Horizon: 76km (48 miles)
Built: July 1938
Historic use: Secondary
Current use: None
Condition: Good

Visibility to other local pillars is excellent, with at least 21 in sight, all round the compass, even across the nearby Hallam, Rud Hill and Burbage moors. On the clearest day, it's well worth taking some time at this pillar to survey the whole horizon.

To leave the Edge, walk back a few metres NW from the pillar to SK 25040 83040, where there is a reasonably easy descent to the path below. From there, it's 500m back to the start, following the worn grass path to the SE, but taking time to look back at the Edge and admire the dramatic rocky outcrops.

Stanage Edge pillar

Pillar	Distance	Direction
Rod Moor	5.5km	NNE (012 deg)
Kirk Edge	10.3km	NNE (015 deg)
Greno Knoll	14.6km	ENNE (030 deg)
Top End	13.1km	ENNE (036 deg)
Ox Stones	2.9km	E (088 deg)
Flask Edge	5.4km	SE (140 deg)
Birchen Edge	10.3km	SSSE (164 deg)
White Edge	7.3km	SSSE (170 deg)
High Rake (damaged)	10.5km	SSW (203 deg)
Sir William Hill	6.1km	WSSW (214 deg)
Abney Moor	7.9km	WSW (243 deg)
Bradwell Moor	12.2km	WWSW (256 deg)
Mam Tor	12.3km	W (273 deg)
Brown Knoll	16.8km	WWNW (277 deg)
Winhill Pike	6.7km	WNW (288 deg)
Edale Moor	13.0km	WNW (291 deg)
West End Moor	15.9km	NW (310 deg)
High Neb	3.3km	NW (316 deg)
Back Tor	9.6km	WNNW (326 deg)
Margery Hill (Primary)	14.1km	NNW (334 deg)
Emlin Ridge *	5.4km	NNW (335 deg)

* The visibility to Emlin Ridge is marginal

Route summary

Your present location	Your next objective	Waypoint at next objective	Directions
Lay-by SK 25330 82580	Stile to lane	SK 25630 82290	400m SE along grass path
SK 25630 82290	Higger Tor summit; the exit point	SK 25650 81940	350m south up to and across the summit
SK 25650 81940	Carl Walk hill fort summit; the exit point	SK 26020 81430	650m SE from Higger Tor, up to and across Carl Walk
SK 26020 81430	Track running below Burbage Edge	SK 26580 81270	500m, first east across a clough, then SE up to track.
SK 26580 81270	Marker post	SK 26780 81490	Go left on track, then 300m NE
SK 26780 81490	Two cairns	SK 27060 81520	280m east through a break in Burbage Edge
SK 27060 81520	Houndkirk Road (track)	SK 27660 81660	600m ENE along moor path
SK 27660 81660	Path crossing track	SK 28610 82640	1.4km NE along track
SK 28610 82640	Path going NNW to pillar	SK 28420 83020	450m NNW by trees
SK 28420 83020	Ox Stones pillar	SK 28021 83134	300m WNW through heather
SK 28021 83134	Ox Stones rocks	SK 27940 83160	100m west from pillar
SK 27940 83160	Gate to lane	SK 27850 83430	350m north through heather
SK 27850 83430	Marker post, three paths to fore	SK 27830 83870	400m north from lane, take right-hand path
SK 27830 83870	Point to turn back WNW	SK 27910 83910	100m NE from post
SK 27910 83910	Stile to farm drive	SK 27750 83960	180m WNW, rough area
SK 27750 83960	Lane, at end of farm drive	SK 27820 84560	600m north through farm
SK 27820 84560	Ladder stile to open moor	SK 27220 84580	500m west, off lane, along track, then field
SK 27220 84580	Point to turn NNW at White Stones – **Key waypoint**	SK 25850 84580	1.5km west (bearing 269 deg), following marked moor path
SK 25850 84580	Point to turn west, then crossing two brooks	SK 25770 84960	400m NNW along moor path
SK 25770 84960	Ladder stile	SK 25610 85020	Take right path after second brook, skirting a fenced area
SK 25610 85020	Stanedge Pole	SK 24680 84420	800m SW on peat path
SK 24680 84420	Stanage Edge	SK 24380 83770	300m SW, wet ground
SK 24380 83770	Robin Hood's Cave	SK 24440 83580	200m SE along Edge
SK 24440 83580	Stanage Edge pillar	SK 25094 83017	1km SE along Edge
SK 25094 83017	Exit from Edge	SK 25040 83040	50m NW from pillar
SK 25040 83040	Back to start Lay-by	SK 25330 82580	500m SE on grass track

Walk 15 – Corbar Hill and Black Edge

Start: Corbar Road, east off the A5004, NW outskirts of Buxton – Map Reference SK 05560 74060

Distance: 14.8km (9.2 miles)

Total ascent: 460m (1690 ft)

Estimated time: 5.5 hours

Grading: Moderate

OS map: Explorer map OL 24 The Peak District – White Peak area

The route

The route takes in the Corbar Hill pillar and Corbar Cross, before making a complete circuit of the Coombs Moss moor, including the pillar on Black Edge, the hill fort at Castle Naze and the dramatic outlook from Coombs Edge. The final leg is a short section of the Midshires Way and A5004 trunk road.

The profile shows a steep climb to the Corbar pillar, but relatively gentle gradients thereafter. There is one steep descent off the moor after 12km.

The walk

From Corbar Road, walk northwards for 10m along the lane marked 'Corbar Woods – Private Lane', entering the wood itself through a brightly coloured fenced access on the right. Continue north for 300m along the woodland path, rising steeply to the top edge of the wood (SK 05370 74260), turning left there (west), following the wall along the top of the wood. After 250m, take the stile (SK 05230 74190) on the right, with a notice declaring Open Access land. From the other side, follow the ruined wall up the grassy bank, crossing a second stile and then climbing the short, but steep section of Corbar Edge. At the top, there is access into the railed area around the cross, but to reach the pillar it's necessary to take the stile over the wall on the right of the enclosure.

Corbar Cross dates back to around 1950, and was presented to the Roman Catholic Church by the Duke of Devonshire. There is no descriptive plaque, so further history regarding the cross is difficult to establish. The Corbar Hill pillar is close by, and predates the cross by about ten years. It remains in excellent condition, with the spider, flush bracket and OS insert all intact.

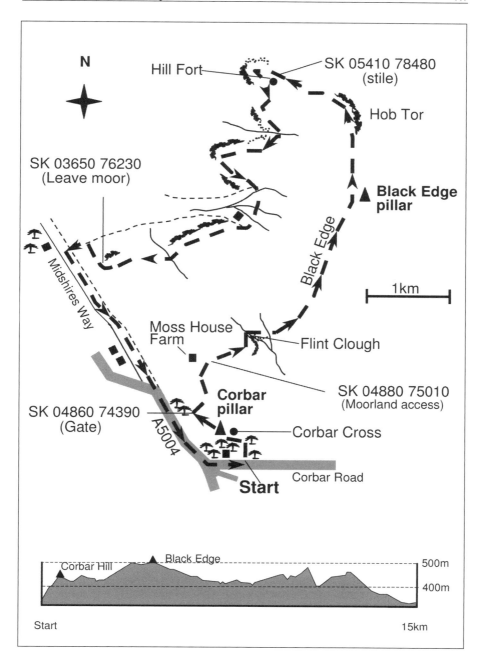

The pillar details are:

Position: SK 05138 74298
Flush bracket No: S2767
Height: 437m (1420 ft)
Horizon: 75km (47 miles)
Built: March 1940
Historic use: Secondary
Current use: None
Condition: Good

Corbar Hill pillar and Corbar Cross

Around 13 local pillars are in view, mostly in the eastern half of the compass, but with four to the SW and south, including the Blake Mere Primary. Wild Moor (Burbage Edge area) restricts visibility to the west, and the western end of Coombs Moss limits views to the north and NE. Surprisingly, there is no line of sight to the other pillar on this walk, Black Edge, only 3km distant to the NNE.

Corbar Hill and the two fields extending to the NNW towards Moss House Farm, right up to the boundary wall with the Coombs Moss moor, are all Open Access. But

Pillar	Distance	Direction
Mam Tor	12.0km	ENNE (039 deg)
Bee Low *	6.4km	NE (040 deg)
Bradwell Moor	9.9km	NENE (053 deg)
Abney Moor	14.0km	ENE (068 deg)
Wormhill	5.7km	EENE (076 deg)
Fairfield	2.6km	E (087 deg)
Wardlow	12.6km	E (091 deg)
Sough Top	8.8km	ESE (112 deg)
Hind Low *	5.9km	ESSE (150 deg)
Blake Mere (Primary)	13.3km	S (184 deg)
Axe Edge	4.0km	SSW (203 deg)
Burbage Edge	2.4km	WSW (244 deg)
Shining Tor	5.7km	WWSW (264 deg)

* Pillars missing

the field immediately to the west of the Lightwood Reservoir plantation, including the Cuckoo Tors, is private, and there is no established right of way from the pillar towards the reservoir. So the route to gain access to the moor must start by going NNW towards the farm.

From the pillar, pick up the worn grass path that continues west from the wall stile, walking 300m to a gate at the corner of a wood (SK 04860 74390). Pass through it, turning north alongside the left-hand side of the fence and walking 100m to a stile over another fence. On the other side, turn NW, following the faint path towards the farm and to the far side of the field, crossing a small stream in the bottom. Then turn NNE, walking uphill towards the wall that marks the boundary with the open moor.

At SK 04880 75010, towards the eastern side of the Open Access area, there is a section of wall that has fallen, guarded by a makeshift gate that is tied to one post by way of a 'hinge', with a looped tie to another post. This can be lifted aside to allow access over the wall and under the high strand of barbed wire, remembering to reposition the gate and secure the tie afterwards. The moor is also Open Access, but with restrictions relating to grouse shooting (including 'no dogs') and land management, so the makeshift gate is a legitimate access from one open area to another. It's obviously well used by walkers and, as always, the principle to observe is one of preserving the security of the boundary and not disturbing any more stones.

From the point of access, follow the north side of the wall, walking NE. The peat and gritstone path through the heather is not marked on most maps, but it is well walked and actually circles the entire moor. For the most part, the majority of the route follows this path, never far from the wall. The first significant obstacle to be encountered is Flint Clough, a stream that feeds the Lightwater Reservoir, at SK 05320 75400. To cross the stream, the path turns NW for 150m, then returns on the other side to resume its progress alongside the wall. From there, it is 2km NNE along Black Edge to the pillar, the ground steadily rising.

The pillar is on the second high point to be encountered, so that when looking back, the first section of the Edge obscures Corbar Hill pillar. The Black Edge pillar is in excellent condition, with all its original features intact, even though the base has been exposed by erosion.

The pillar details are:

Position: SK 06254 77006
Flush bracket No: S2775
Height: 507m (1648 ft)
Horizon: 81km (50 miles)
Built: April 1940
Historic use: Secondary
Current use: None
Condition: Good

Black Edge pillar

Visibility to other local pillar sites is exceptional, embracing at least 23 locations all round the compass. The best views are to the south and east, across the A6 trunk road, covering the entire area of Buxton and the Peak National Park. To the NE, the scarred landscape of Bee Low quarry (where the pillar was lost to the excavations) is evident in the foreground, with views towards Mam Tor and Kinder Scout beyond that.

From the pillar, continue NNE along the wall, the route steadily turning north as it skirts the rocky outcrop at Hob Tor (SK 06290 77750), then NW as it approaches Short Edge. At SK 06220 78030 there is a choice of paths, one keeping closer to the edge, the other cutting the corner across the heather moor, both converging again at SK 06000 78180. From there, the path follows the edge, overlooking the valley to the north, crossing a fallen wall before reaching the hill fort at Castle Naze.

As hill forts go, the Castle Naze hill fort is a modest feature, with parallel ramparts running NE-SW. It's worth a few minutes at the site to consider how it might have been used, perhaps being a place of retreat, taking just a few essential supplies, rather than being a permanent camp. Although the name (meaning 'Castle on a high nose of land') conjures a picture of a stone structure, in its day it would more likely have been a wooden palisade surrounding a group of huts, perhaps with a crude observation tower. Defence on three sides would have been relatively easy, but what about marauders coming from

Pillar	Distance	Direction and bearing
Kinder Low	10.2km	NNNE (009 deg)
Brown Knoll	8.4km	NNNE (014 deg)
Edale Moor	12.7km	ENNE (031 deg)
Mam Tor	9.2km	NE (044 deg)
Bee Low *	3.8km	NENE (055 deg)
Bradwell Moor	7.6km	ENE (065 deg)
Abney Moor	12.0km	EENE (078 deg)
Sir William Hill	15.2km	E (086 deg)
Wheston	7.7km	E (093 deg)
Wardlow	12.1km	EESE (104 deg)
Wormhill	4.7km	ESE (107 deg)
Sough Top	9.3km	SE (130 deg)
Fairfield	3.0km	ESSE (149 deg)
Hind Low *	8.1km	SSSE (167 deg)
Hollinsclough Moor	11.2km	S (183 deg)
Blake Mere (Primary)	16.1km	SSSW (187 deg)
Axe Edge	6.9km	SSW (203 deg)
Burbage Edge	5.0km	SW (221 deg)
Shining Tor	7.5km	WSW (244 deg)
Sponds Hill	9.8km	WNW (289 deg)
Ladder Hill	3.9km	NWNW (298 deg)
Chinley Churn	7.2km	NNW (337 deg)

the SE, across the moor? Maybe, 3000 years ago, the terrain was even more hostile than it is now, discouraging even the most determined attacker.

From the hill fort, take the stile at SK 05410 78480, accessing a path that follows the right-hand side of the wall. To the NW, after 150m, there is a path descending steeply to the lane below, whilst from the top there are expanding views across the Coombs Reservoir (NW) and towards Ladder Hill (WNW), with its own OS pillar and distinctive communication mast. Ignore the path that descends to the lane, turning south instead and following the well-used edge path along the wall. It begins a long walk along the full length of Coombs Edge, the path meandering around the stream valleys and above the dramatic rocky outcrops that constitute the Edge itself.

The first stream to be encountered is Pygreave Brook, where the path crosses the stream at SK 05500 77730 before it turns back from SE to NW on the other side. After about 50m, the path changes direction again, to SW, passing along the top of more rocky outcrops, with a view over Allstone Lee, before veering SE into a broad inlet, revealing new vistas to the SW and the way ahead along the Edge. At the next brook (SK 05320 77150, one of three tributaries of the Meveril Brook that feeds Coombs reservoir), a track joins from the right, coming up from Allstone Lee, the path then turning south around the inlet and meeting the second tributary at SK 05270 76870. Alongside the third tributary, at SK 05160

76800, there is a small stone shelter that can offer some respite in harsh weather. Nearby is a second hut, well secured, probably serving the grouse shoots in late summer.

Shooting hut

Leaving the stone huts in a westerly direction, ignore the distinctive path that drops down below the edge, continuing instead along the left (south) of the wall. After 800m, the route crosses two more brooks, set only 50m apart, producing some very boggy areas, before veering west for 600m, still following the wall. At SK 03820 76400, the path veers SW again, following the edge for another 250m.

At SK 03650 76230, the path reaches the point where the boundary wall turns left (SE). Turn right at this point, leaving the moor, using the faint path that descends steeply NW for 300m, continuing across Open Access land. The path follows a range-wire fence, crosses a makeshift stile at SK 03550 76390 and finally joins a public footpath running along the bottom (SK 03470 76510) on the other side of a second stile. There, go left, following the right-hand side of a wall for 200m until reaching a stile on to the Midshires Way, with the White Hall Activity Centre on the other side of the lane. It's an establishment that specialises in a wide range of training courses, centred on outdoor pursuits, including climbing and advanced navigation.

Turn left (SE) along the Midshires Way, following the metalled road and sandstone track for 2km until it reaches the A5004 trunk road, then continue SE. The route along the road is reasonable walking; the traffic is usually light, there's a wide pavement, and it comes of something of a relief after such a long period of moorland paths. On the way, there's a well-preserved millstone to admire, a symbol of the Peak District National Park, set in wall-side display.

Finally, after 1.5km on the main road, turn left into Corbar road, where it's about 250m back to the Corbar Woods entrance and the parking area.

Route summary

Your present location	Your next objective	Waypoint at next objective	Directions
Corbar Road SK 05560 74060	Top of Corbar Woods	SK 05370 74260	300m north, into wood and along woodland path
SK 05370 74260	Stile to Open Access land	SK 05230 74190	250m west along top of wood
SK 05230 74190	Corbar Hill pillar and Corbar Cross	SK 05138 74298	150m NE, through Corbar Edge
SK 05138 74298	Gate, by corner of wood	SK 04860 74390	300m WNW, grass path
SK 04860 74390	Stile	SK 04910 74510	130m NNE along fence
SK 04910 74510	Stream crossing	SK 04750 74680	230m NW, grass path
SK 04750 74680	Point of access to moor, makeshift gate in wall	SK 04880 75010	300m NNE, across marshy area and up to the boundary wall
SK 04880 75010	Flint Clough	SK 05320 75400	600m NE, moor path by wall
SK 05320 75400	Black Edge pillar	SK 06254 77006	2km NNE, moor path by wall
SK 06254 77006	Hob Tor rocky outcrop	SK 06290 77750	800m north, moor path
SK 06290 77750	Short Edge	SK 06220 78030	300m NNW, moor path
SK 06220 78030	Fallen wall, nearing Castle Naze hill fort	SK 05700 78330	600m NW, moor path
SK 05700 78330	Stile to right of wall, leaving hill fort	SK 05410 78480	300m west by hill fort
SK 05410 78480	Pygreave Brook	SK 05500 77730	1km SSE along edge path
SK 55500 77730	Rocky outcrop overlooking Allstone Lee	SK 04920 77480	800m SW along edge path
SK 04920 77480	Stream crossing	SK 05320 77150	600m SE along edge path
SK 05320 77150	Second stream crossing	SK 05270 76870	300m south, edge path
SK 05270 76870	Third stream and shooting hut	SK 05160 76800	150m SW on edge path, keep left of wall after the hut
SK 05160 76800	Stream crossing	SK 04400 76400	900m SW, moor path by wall
SK 04400 76400	Point where moor path veers SW	SK 03820 76400	600m west, moor path by wall
SK 03820 76400	Point to leave the moor	SK 03650 76230	250m SW, by wall
SK 03650 76230	Stile to public footpath	SK 03470 76510	450m NW, after a steep descent
SK 03470 76510	Stile accessing Midshires Way	SK 03340 76380	200m SW, grass path by wall
SK 03340 76380	A5004 trunk road	SK 04320 74770	2km SE on Midshires Way
SK 04320 74770	Entry into Corbar Road	SK 05430 73870	1.5km SE along A5004
SK 05430 73870	Start, in Corbar road	SK 05560 74060	250m NE on road

Walk 16 – Flask Edge and White Edge

Start: At the Longshaw National Trust car park near the junction of the A625 and the B6054 – Map Reference SK 26620 79040

Distance: 15km (9.4 miles)

Total ascent: 280m (900ft)

Estimated time: 4.5 hours

Grading: Easy to moderate

OS map: Explorer Map OL 24 – The Peak District – White Peak

The Route

The route crosses Totley Moss and Big Moor using well-trodden paths, first visiting the Flask Edge pillar and then going on to the Barbrook reservoir and the Barbrook stone circles. The return leg is along White Edge, visiting the pillar, then north back to the car park.

The profile shows only modest gradients, with a gentle downhill ending. Whilst the Flask Edge trig is on a prominent peak, the White Edge pillar is positioned specifically for its views westwards across the edge.

The walk

Walk to the northern end of the car park, exiting through a wall stile and turning north along a grassy path, continuing for 300m to a set of stone steps (SK 26640 79400) that lead to the road above. Once across the road, the route follows a wide track eastwards across Totley Moss, towards a railway tunnel vent. Passing to the south of the vent, walk a further 600m, locating a single spar of fencing on the right, at SK 28390 79380. It's engraved with a 'No Vehicles' warning and it marks the best route south up to the Flask Edge pillar and beyond. It is probably one of the tracks left behind when gas pipes were laid through the area, but it is now used as a path in preference to the older rights of way.

As the route approaches the pillar, there is a cairn 300m due east. On some maps it is indicated as an ancient 'enclosure' (for sheep, mostly), one of many such features that are evident in the Peak District area. They date back to the Bronze or Iron Age, with the new farmers of that time marking their boundaries with wooden palisades. But that particular enclosure has been modernised with some corrugated iron sheets! Later in the walk, as seen from White Edge, those same farmers have left buried signs of their old field systems, more evident to the archaeologist than to the walker, but there none the less.

The Flask Edge pillar is in reasonable condition, with the spider intact and the original OS plug still in place, but with some erosion of the concrete.

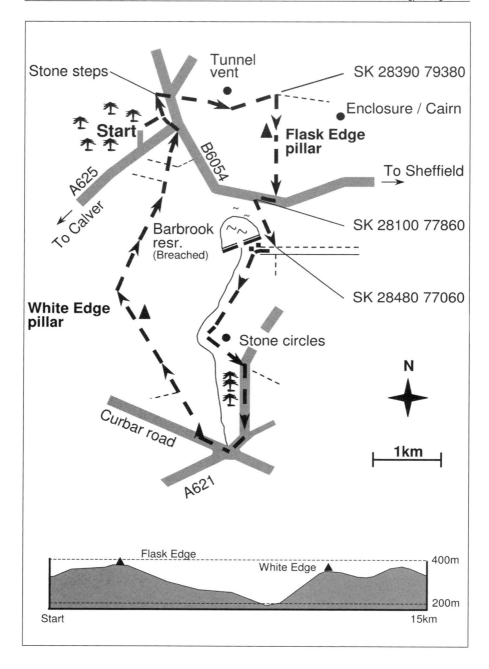

The pillar details are:

Position: SK 28492 78842
Flush bracket No: S2131
Height: 395m (1284 ft)
Horizon: 71km (44 miles)
Built: June 1938
Historic use: Secondary
Current use: None
Condition: Fair

Flask Edge pillar

The pillar has excellent views all round, and triangulates with at least 15 others, including the Primary trig at Harland South. Interestingly, the two closest pillars at Totley and Blacka Plantation are not in sight. To the west is the distinctive Sir William Hill, and to the north and NW there is visibility to Stanage Edge and Mam Tor.

From the pillar, regain the pipeline track that brought the route to the summit; there's a conspicuous white gas pole to the south marking the starting point. Follow the track down to the road (B6054) and then turn westwards. After 400m, look for a gate on the left of the lane, at SK 28100 77860; it's the access to a wide grassy path that

Pillar	Distance	Direction
Ringing Low	5.0km	NNE (017 deg)
Northern Common	4.6km	E (086 deg)
Coal Aston	7.2km	E (086 deg)
Grange Hill	6.1km	ESSE (150 deg)
Harland South (Primary)	10.8km	SSSE (172 deg)
Birchen Edge	5.8km	SSSW (187 deg)
Calton Pastures	11.7km	SSW (204 deg)
White Edge	3.4 km	WSSW (216 deg)
High Rake (damaged)	9.4km	SWSW (235 deg)
Wardlow	11.7km	WSW (246 deg)
Sir William Hill	7.0km	WWSW (263 deg)
Abney Moor	10.4km	W (274 deg)
Mam Tor	16.4km	WNW (287 deg)
Stanage Edge	5.4km	WNNW (321 deg)
Ox Stones	4.3km	NNNW (354 deg)

circles round to the Barbrook Reservoir. Any other tracks from the road to the reservoir can be extremely wet, even in summer. Take the grassy track due south for 500m, and then bear right at a fork in the path (SK 28450 77410). On the way, the route passes within 200m of the Barbrook III stone circle at SK 28290 77340, which is now no more than a rubble bank and a dry-stone wall. Leave it be; there are better circles to look at later. Instead, follow the path down to a metalled drive at SK 28480 77060, turning west at that point and arriving at the SE corner of the reservoir.

Here, it's worth a look at the remains of the reservoir by walking along the top of the dam. It's an Open Access area, and a popular spot for bird watching, but the dam has been breached, releasing most of the water. Apparently, this bizarre measure was taken because the cost of meeting the European Union standards for reservoir status was considered too high. It seems that the bureaucrats didn't think of erecting a simple notice saying 'This is not a Reservoir' and preserving a pleasant mere for the greater benefit of the local wildlife.

Barbrook I stone circle

The best view of the breach comes when walking on, following the track to the SW (starting by the finger post at SK 28230 76970), and then looking back at the dam. This pleasant track eventually turns SE and, near SK 27840 75600, passes 100m to the west of the Barbrook I stone circle. It is one of the best-preserved features of its kind in the Peak District and, as with many of the circles, has been the subject of much study and speculation.

Like the enclosures, the circle dates back three or four thousand years to the Bronze Age farmers. But why did they build such features? Some researchers believe that they are the very first attempts at monitoring the phases of the sun and the moon, perhaps as an early form of triangulation. As the very first farmers to inhabit the area, those people would certainly have been interested in formally tracking the seasons, so that sowing and reaping could be properly planned. They didn't have our present day advantage of knowledge about the solar system; nor did they have calendars or any absolute understanding of the length of a year.

One theory says that if you stand in the centre of the circle, then the sun and moon will rise and set over certain stones at the various equinoxes. A cynic might say that, depending where you make the centre, such coincidences can be produced at will, so that the circle might just as well have been a meeting place, perhaps for worship. Crucially, the fact that the 'circle' is not round, but a slight 'D' shape, makes the positioning of the centre somewhat uncertain.

It is a debate that will go on, and for those who wish to visit another fine example of Peak District circles, the best is certainly the henge at Arbor Low (SK 16030 63580, near Parsley Hay). And finally, to visit the Barbrook II circle, it is just 250m NW from the Barbrook I circle, at SK 27750 75820. Follow the faint path north from Barbrook I to a dome-shaped grass and rock mound (possibly a burial chamber), then west to the second circle. It is a well-preserved rubble feature, with an entrance and with small standing stones distributed around the circumference.

Having had your fill of stone circles, retrace the route back to the main track and continue SE, emerging on to the A621. Follow the main road south, then SW to the crossroads, turning right (WNW) along the minor road towards Curbar. The verges are wide, so that the road walking is not unpleasant. There are no viable alternatives, not even in the fields to the west side of the road. The stile to re-enter the moorland area is 200m from the crossroads, on the right-hand side of the road at SK 27660 74100, set into the wall. The route then heads NW across grassy moors along a well-defined path, before rising towards the White Edge summit.

The White Edge pillar is positioned on a high point of Big Moor, with excellent views across the Froggatt and Curbar Edges to the west. It's in good condition, painted white, with the spider intact. The original plug has been replaced with a stone insert.

White Edge pillar

The pillar details are:

Position: SK 26378 75855
Flush bracket No: S2132
Height: 365m (1186 ft)
Horizon: 68km (43 miles)
Built: June 1938
Historic use: Secondary
Current use: None
Condition: Good

The pillar triangulates with about 12 others, including the Primary at Harland South, mostly to the north, west and south. Views to the east tend to be blocked by Big Moor itself.

From the White Edge pillar, the way home is straightforward, the path leading north for 200m, then NW for 500m, and finally NE for the last 2.5km.

Pillar	Distance	Direction
Flask Edge	3.7km	ENNE (036 deg)
Grange Hill	5.6km	ESE (114 deg)
Birchen Edge	3.1km	SSE (153 deg)
Harland South (Primary)	8.6km	SSE (155 deg)
Calton Pastures	8.1km	SSW (199 deg)
High Rake (damaged)	6.0km	WSW (246 deg)
Wardlow	8.7km	WWSW (258 deg)
Wheston	12.5km	W (274 deg)
Sir William Hill	5.2km	WNW (293 deg)
Winhill Pike	12.0km	WNNW (321 deg)
High Neb	10.1km	NNW (340 deg)
Stanage Edge	7.3km	NNNW (350 deg)

On the way, two other paths cross the route, both of which lead down to the main road. One is at SK 26630 77820 (there's a signpost by the wall) and the other is at SK 26680 78420, but the best policy is to keep straight on and emerge over the stile at the road junction between the A625 and the B6054. Cross that junction and take the track to the NW, turning SW to reach the wall-stile that leads back into the car park.

Route summary

Your present location	Your next objective	Waypoint at next objective	Directions
Start, car park SK 26620 79040	Bottom of stone steps.	SK 26640 79400	Leave car park at stile, then 250m NNW
SK 26640 79400	The tunnel vent, passing to its south	SK 27730 79330	Follow the track 1km east from the road
SK 27730 79330	'No Vehicles' sign. Then turn south up the track	SK 28390 79380	600m ENE from the vent
SK 28390 79380	Flask Edge pillar. The ancient enclosure is to the east	SK 28492 78842	600m SSE from the sign to the pillar
SK 28492 78842	Down to the road (B6054)	SK 28540 77790	1km south on the same 'gas track' that came up to the pillar
SK 28540 77790	Gate for the grassy path	SK 28100 77860	400m west. The road is not busy
SK 28100 77860	A fork in the grassy path	SK 28450 77410	500m SSE, go right (south) at this fork
SK 28450 77410	Metalled drive to Barbrook reservoir	SK 28480 77060	300m south Then turn west to inspect the reservoir itself
Finger post at SK 28230 76970	Barbrook I stone circle, just NE of the track	SK 27840 75600	1.7km SW, then south, then SE
Note that the Barbrook II stone circle is NW of the Barbrook I circle, at SK 27750 75820			
SK 27840 75600	The main road (A621)	SK 28110 75140	500m south and SE along the track from the circles
SK 28110 75140	Cross roads	SK 27810 74020	1.3km south. There, turn right towards Curbar
SK 27810 74020	Stile in the north wall of Curbar road,	SK 27660 74100	200m WNW, leading to the path to White Edge
SK 27660 74100	White Edge pillar	SK 26378 75855	2.3km NW. The pillar is 50m east of the path
SK 26378 75855	Point where the path veers from NW to NE	SK 26000 76500	800m NW from the pillar
SK 26000 76500	Road junction, A625 and B6054	SK 26830 78960	2.5km of easy walking, generally NNE
SK 26830 78960	Back to the car park	SK 26620 79040	300m. Cross to the track, walk NW, then west

Walk 17 – Shining Tor and Burbage Edge

Start: Pym Chair car park, lane from the A537 Macclesfield to Buxton road – Map reference SJ 99460 76770

Distance: 16km (10.0 miles)

Total ascent: 620m (2000 ft)

Estimated time: 5 hours

Grading: Moderate to strenuous

OS map: Explorer Map OL 24 The Peak District – White Peak area

The Route

In the main, the route follows established paths, descending the Goyt valley twice, so that the cumulative ascent makes for a challenging walk. There is a pleasant mixture of open moorland, wooded areas, a disused railway and some road walking around the reservoirs. Navigation is relatively straightforward.

The route height profile shows the two descents across the Goyt valley, so the total ascent is 620m. Both pillars are on local high spots, either side of the Goyt valley.

The walk

From the Pym Chair car park, walk south up to the crest of the road, passing an information board on the way. It seems that Pym was either a preacher or a robber, which seems to cover the whole spectrum of possible characters. If it's the same 'Pym', he has another chair, a rock situated on the top of the Kinder plateau, overlooking the Jacob's Ladder ascent from the Edale valley.

At the crest of the road, take the stile, walking due south across Oldgate Nick and along the ridge towards the first high point, Cats Tor. The views to the west are excellent, and the onward walking up to the Shining Tor summit is straightforward, following the east side of the wall all the way. The path is increasingly paved, so that the once boggy areas are now greatly reduced. To the east are the wooded areas that embrace the Goyt valley. It is from there that the route returns at the end of the walk.

Shining Tor is the highest point in Cheshire, with splendid views all round. The pillar is well looked after, positioned just the other side of a wall from the path, with a stile exclusively erected for easy access. It is regularly repainted. The spider and flush bracket are intact, but the original OS insert has been replaced by a plastic plug.

The pillar triangulates with at least 14 local pillar sites; with views all round the compass. To the SSW is the distinctive Shutlingsloe summit, sometimes

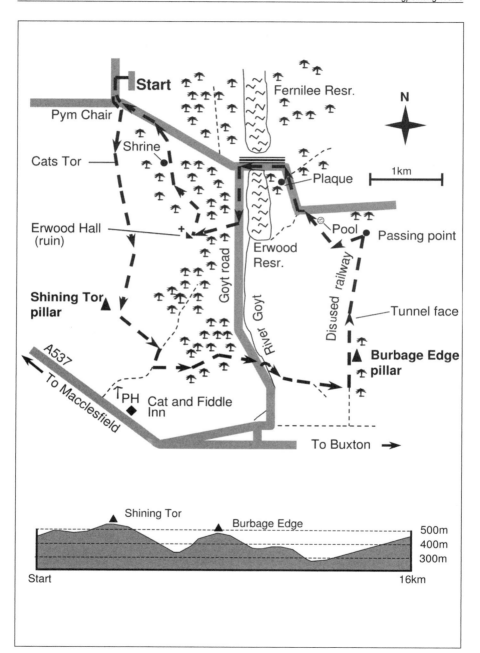

called the 'Cheshire Matterhorn'. The pillar on Croker Hill (to the SW, with its distinctive BT tower) has long since gone, knocked over when the tower was being constructed. Likewise, the pillar at Hind Low to the SE is no longer standing; that one was lost some years ago to the expanding quarry. To the WNW, between the Kerridge Hill and Nab Head summits, the distinctive white folly called 'White Nancy' is clearly visible. Eastwards is Burbage Edge, sporting the second pillar on this walk.

The pillar details are:

Position: SJ 99463 73739
Flush bracket No: S2773
Height: 559m (1817 ft)
Horizon: 85km (53 miles)
Built: April 1940
Historic use: Secondary
Current use: None
Condition: Good

Shining Tor pillar

From the pillar, follow the path SE across Shooters Clough valley, indicated to the Cat and Fiddle. Turn south at the stile on the other side of the valley, and then east after the next stile gate, at SK 00060 72970, signposted to Goyt's Clough Quarry. This is the point on the walk where the route crosses from the British Grid 'SJ' square to 'SK'.

There is then a fairly steep descent into the Goyt valley, the rock-strewn path crossing Stake Clough before it enters the woodland. It emerges briefly to cross a wooden bridge over Deep Clough, be-

Pillar	Distance	Direction
Chinley Churn	10.7km	NNE (022 deg)
Ladder Hill	6.1km	ENNE (033 deg)
Black Edge	7.5km	ENE (064 deg)
Corbar Hill	5.7km	EENE (084 deg)
Burbage Edge	3.5km	EESE (098 deg)
Hind Low *	9.9km	SESE (119 deg)
Axe Edge	5.1km	SESE (128 deg)
The Roaches	9.9km	S (176 deg)
Gun	12.5km	SSSW (191 deg)
Shutlingsloe	4.5km	SSW (204 deg)
Croker Hill *	8.6km	SW (225 deg)
Kerridge Hill	5.7km	WNW (293 deg)
Nab Head	7.4km	NW (313 deg)
Sponds Hill	7.0km	NNW (339 deg)

* Pillars destroyed

fore again entering the wood. After finally emerging, follow the finger post marked 'Derbyshire Bridge' for some 15m and then bear left down a diagonal grass path leading to the Goyt valley lane and the River Goyt (SK 01530 72950). Cross the bridge over the river, following the path signposted to Buxton. This narrow path through the heather leads up to a fork at SK 02620 72700. Keep left there, continuing for another 300m up to Burbage Edge. At the fence, turn north towards the pillar, 600m distant. The path is often boggy, and the zigzag detours around the wettest parts are all part of the challenge. But keep close to the fence wherever possible.

Like the one on Shining Tor, the pillar is in good condition and well looked after. But it has more limited views, the Shining Tor ridge itself blocking the line-of-sight to pillars in the west. To the north, east and south, about nine pillar sites are in view, including the site of the missing one at the Hind Low quarry to the SE.

The pillar details are:

Position: SK 02960 73247
Flush bracket No: S4232
Height: 500m (1625 ft)
Horizon: 80km (50 miles)
Built: September 1947
Historic use: Secondary
Current use: None
Condition: Good

Burbage Edge pillar

From the pillar, continue north. It's a steep descent, the path following the fence down to the disused railway. In wet conditions it can be very tricky, particularly the last 50m. At the bottom, the first evidence of the disused railway is a sealed tunnel entrance at SK 03080 74130. This was the old Cromford and High Peak Railway that dated back to 1831, and in its heyday it boasted 33 miles of track with no

Pillar	Distance	Direction
Black Edge	5.0km	NE (041 deg)
Corbar Hill	2.4km	ENE (064 deg)
Wormhill	8.1km	ENE (073 deg)
Fairfield	4.9km	EENE (076 deg)
Sough Top	10.6km	EESE (103 deg)
Hind Low *	6.7km	SE (130 deg)
Axe Edge	2.7km	SSSE (168 deg)
Shining Tor	3.5km	WWNW (278 deg)
Ladder Hill	5.6km	N (358 deg)

* Pillar destroyed

less than nine steep hills to test the steam locomotives, the most severe being the Hopton incline. The line was distinguished as being the steepest in Britain (seven percent, overall), and boasted the tightest single curve, the 55-yard radius curve at Gotham. The line closed in 1967.

The tunnel is sealed for reasons of safety, so entry is forbidden. To the south, the route of the disused railway emerges again from the other end of the tunnel just before the A54 Buxton to Macclesfield road, and the remnants of the bridge across that road are still evident. From there, the southerly route of the old track is intermittent, but is very evident again around the area of Parsley Hay, where it is established as the High Peak Trail.

To continue the walk, from the tunnel entrance, follow the disused railway north, winding around the hillsides. The views and the walking are excellent. As the route later turns westwards, with a passing point for the trains, it's clear that a great deal of material was moved in order to construct the embankments. Finally, the track turns back NW and emerges on to the road by a small pool that was used to supply water for the engines (at SK 02340 75160).

The old railway then followed the route taken by the lane down to the dam, this section having been abandoned in 1892 when new routes and more powerful engines were introduced. Before that, it required a stationary engine to haul the trains up the steep 14 percent Bunsall Incline. At the bottom (Bunsall Cob), there is a roadside plaque explaining more of the local history. After that, turn west, crossing the dam that creates the Errwood reservoir, the water source for a greater part of the Manchester and Stockport areas. It was inaugurated in 1968.

On the other side of the dam, turn south, following the road for 800m. Cross over a bridge and veer SE towards the large car park and picnic area on the right (west). Turn west just before that parking area, using a diagonal path across the verge that leaves from SK 01180 74960. Then locate the swing barrier at SK 01050 74850 marking the start of a path through the rhododendrons to the old ruin of Errwood Hall. After 200m along that path there is a short, steep incline, the route doubling back to the right (north) just before reaching the top, then following a path that emerges by the ruin.

The hall was built in the mid-1800s by the wealthy Grimshawe family. They were shipping merchants from Manchester who enjoyed a life of luxury, with riches flowing in from their trade in cotton, coal and paper exports, so that they were able to build themselves a fine yacht and sail the world. When the family died out in 1930, the hall spent a short period as a youth hostel before being demolished to avoid any risk of pollution to the new Fernilee Reservoir. It is difficult to see how such pollution could have occurred, but maybe the intention was for a deeper reservoir system than eventually emerged.

From the ruin, take the path that leaves around the north side of the site, following it westwards. Having crossed a long footbridge (SK 00640 74870), the path back to the car branches off to the NW. But before taking that route, consider a visit the Errwood Hall cemetery, which is on the high ground to the south, when standing on the bridge. The best approach is by walking round the west side of the hill, where there is a diagonal path up the steep slope.

The homeward path from the hall

Miss Dolores' shrine

grounds on to the lane that leads back to Pym Chair is straightforward, skirting the woodland, with good views back up to the Shining Tor ridge. Before reaching the road there is one last feature to visit; that is a curious shrine, at SK 00240 75920. It was dedicated to a certain Miss Dolores, a member of Spanish nobility who returned to England with the Grimshawes after one of their many jaunts abroad. Whether she was governess, friend or mistress is unknown, but whoever she was, she merited a very personal memorial. Take a look inside, it's always open to the walking public and it's still used for Parish communications. But beware; it can be very claustrophobic.

After that brief spiritual experience, continue on the path, emerging on to the lane, leaving 500m of steep up-hill road walking back to the Pym Chair car park.

Route summary

Your present location	Your next objective	Waypoint at next objective	Directions
Pym Chair car park SJ 99460 76770	Stile at Pym Chair summit	SJ 99560 76720	Walk south and then east along the lane
SJ 99560 76720	Shining Tor pillar	SJ 99463 73739	3km south along the wall, over Cats Tor
SJ 99463 73739	Stile gate, signposted to Goyt's Clough Quarry	SK 00060 72970	1km SE and then south from the pillar
SK 00060 72970	Goyt river and bridge	SK 01530 72950	2km generally east, via Stake Side wood
SK 01530 72950	Fork in path, alongside Berry Clough	SK 02620 72700	1km east. Keep left at this fork
SK 02620 72700	The fence on Burbage Edge	SK 02950 72660	300m east. Turn north at the fence
SK 02950 72660	Burbage Edge pillar	SK 02960 73247	600m north, boggy ground
SK 02960 73247	Disused railway, sealed tunnel entrance	SK 03080 74130	1km north, at the bottom of a steep incline. Tricky when wet
SK 03080 74130	Lane, by the watering pool	SK 02340 75160	Follow the disused railway for 2km
SK 02340 75160	Road junction, west side of the dam	SK 01350 75680	Follow the lane down and across the dam for 1.5km Then turn left along the reservoir
SK 01350 75680	Car park	SK 01180 74960	800m south along the road.
SK 01180 74960	Swing barrier across the track that goes to the ruin	SK 01050 74850	150m SW into the wooded area
SK 01050 74850	Point to double back to the right	SK 00830 74740	200m SW, uphill through the rhododendrons
SK 00830 74740	The ruin	SK 00800 74840	100m NW
SK 00800 74840	Footbridge, marking the way to the homeward path, cemetery to south	SK 00640 74870	Walk 100m around the north side of the ruin site.
SK 00640 74870	Miss Dolores' shrine	SK 00240 75920	1.3km NW along the path, skirting the woods
SK 00240 75920	Lane	SK 00180 76150	300m north from the shrine
SK 00180 76150	Car park	SJ 99460 76770	600m NW on lane, over Pym Chair summit and back to the car park

Walk 18 – Shutlingsloe, taking in Tegg's Nose

Start: Roadside pull-off, within 300m NNE of 'The Crag' Inn at Wildboarclough – Map Reference SJ 98270 68730

Distance: 15.3km (9.5 miles)

Total ascent: 700m (2275ft)

Estimated time: 5.5 hours

Grading: Moderate to strenuous

OS map: Explorer map OL 24 The Peak District – White Peak area

The route

The route rises quickly out of Wildboarclough up to the Shutlingsloe summit, then drops down through Macclesfield Forest and passes a series of reservoirs before taking in the Tegg's Nose Country Park. Return is via the north of the forest and down to the Wildboarclough valley along the lanes.

The height profile shows three significant climbs, so that the total ascent is nearly 700m. The climb up Shutlingsloe is particularly steep.

The walk

From the roadside pull-off, walk SSW along the road, passing the bridge over Clough Brook, with its plaque commemorating the flood disaster of 1989. The stream looks innocent enough, but on 24th May of that year, a ferocious thunderstorm over the moors to the NE unleashed a torrent of water that funnelled down the valley, demolishing the bridge, sweeping aside cars and causing a fatality. It was all over in a couple of hours, but nature had made its point.

Continue SSW for 100m, turning right (due north) into a drive marked 'Private' and 'Walkers only'. Walk up the hill as far as the perimeter wall of Shutlingsloe Farm, then turn west, following the path towards the Shutlingsloe summit. It's a very challenging climb, and near the top it is particularly steep. Shutlingsloe is often called the 'Cheshire Matterhorn', but not because of its profile as seen from this easterly approach. The similarity is better appreciated later in the walk when the summit is seen from the north, but even so, the comparison with the famous Swiss mountain is a little generous.

The pillar is in reasonable condition, but its OS plug has been lost. There is a small geographic information plaque nearby and the summit is an extremely popular spot with walkers. As a consequence, erosion control has been a priority for many years, protecting the pillar as well as the terrain around it.

The pillar triangulates with about 11 others nearby, further views being

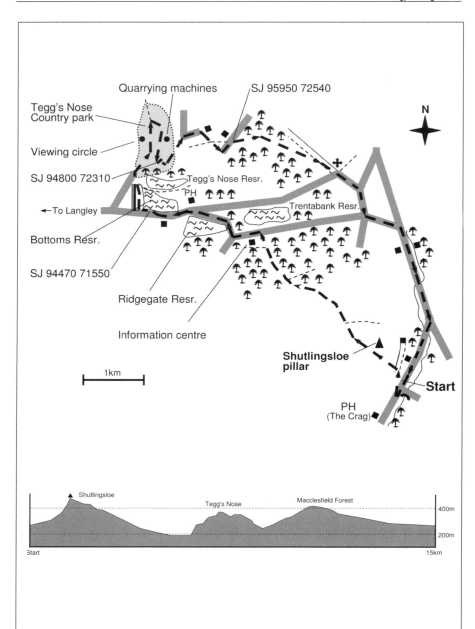

Quarrying machines

SJ 95950 72540

Tegg's Nose
Country park

N

Viewing circle

SJ 94800 72310

Tegg's Nose Resr.

PH

←To Langley

Trentabank Resr.

Bottoms Resr.

SJ 94470 71550

Ridgegate Resr.

Information centre

Shutlingsloe
pillar

1km

PH
(The Crag)

Start

Shutlingsloe

Tegg's Nose

Macclesfield Forest

400m

200m

Start

15km

blocked by the Shining Tor ridge to the NE, Dane Bower to the east (which nearly cuts off the view to Axe Edge) and Macclesfield Forest to the NW.

The pillar details are:

Position: SJ 97645 69574
Flush bracket No: S2760
Height: 506m (1645 ft)
Horizon: 80km (50 miles)
Built: April 1940
Historic use: Secondary
Current use: None
Condition: Fair

Shutlingsloe pillar

From the pillar, descend the flight of stone steps on the NNW side of the hill. Whilst they are much appreciated, they can be very slippery in icy conditions. They lead on to a neatly laid trail of paving stones that ease the way for the next 1km across some very boggy ground, eventually entering Macclesfield Forest at SJ 97170 70350. In the forest,

Pillar	Distance	Direction
Shining Tor	4.5km	NNE (023 deg)
Axe Edge **	6.0km	E (090 deg)
Blake Mere (Primary)	10.8km	ESSE (142 deg)
The Roaches	6.2km	SSE (156 deg)
Gun	8.1km	S (184 deg)
High Bent	11.9km	WSSW (210 deg)
The Cloud	9.3km	SW (230 deg)
Croker Hill *	4.6km	WSW (246 deg)
New Farm	9.0km	WNW (289 deg)
Blakelow	5.1km	NWNW (303 deg)
Sponds Hill	10.8km	N (356 deg)

* Pillar destroyed   ** The visibility to Axe Edge is marginal

turn west and follow the limestone track for 1.2km in a generally NW direction, always taking the path that is signposted to 'Trentabank'.

It's a pleasant walk, and you may be lucky enough to see one of the herd of red deer that populate the area, or even a heron on the Trentabank Reservoir. Indeed, it boasts the largest heronry in the Peak District. Be aware, however, that it is a working forest with tree-felling and planting activities that might occasionally close one of the paths. If that happens, diversion signs are usually posted to indicate the temporary changes.

Emerging on to the lane, opposite Trentabank Reservoir, turn left (west) and walk 400m to the next junction, passing the tourist information centre on the way. Follow the road to the right at the junction and walk around the east side of Ridgegate Reservoir, arriving at the 'Leather's Smithy' public house. It's a fine hostelry, with a theme of classic motoring and rambling, tempting trigpointers in for mid-walk refreshment.

Turn left at the pub, walking 800m towards Langley and the curiously named Bottoms Reservoir. It's now that there are the first good views of the scarred Tegg's Nose hill to the north. Enter the area of the Bottoms Reservoir at the sign-

Higher Blakelow

post for the 'Gritstone Way' (SJ 94470 71550), walking NE along the top of the dam and then turning north along the next dam, across the top of 'Tegg's Nose' reservoir.

Entry to the country park is on the left of the small car park, marked by an ornate wrought iron gate. The path follows a long flight of steps, passing through a wooded area and emerging into open grassland. It's a steady climb, but there are strategically positioned seats for those who want to pause for a while and admire the view. At the top, after a short set of stone steps, a gate (at SJ 94740 72300) marks the entrance to the track that circles the Tegg's Nose summit. Turn left there (NNW), walk 200m to the next gate, turn back ESE along the track for 100m and finally turn north again just before the next gate. That path leads up to a viewing point, with a 'Skylark's View' information board describing the panoramic landscape to the west.

Looking west from the viewpoint, the hill in the immediate foreground is Higher Blakelow, with an OS pillar on the high point. From the position by the tourist board, the pillar is 1.4km distant on a 266 deg bearing (nearly due west). It can be easily seen with binoculars, next to a wall and, probably, with a great deal of building materials around it. It's on private land, and we don't suggest a visit as part of this walk. However, it's included later in the section on 'Drive-by visits'. But why was a pillar erected there, with such restricted views to the east, when Tegg's Nose itself would have been a much better site? The answer probably lies in the quarrying activities on Tegg's Nose; any pillar placed there was likely to come under threat from excavation.

Quarrying machinery

From that viewing point, walk uphill again in a northerly direction to another unusual feature. It's a stone-walled circle with a series of spy-ports, each with a name describing the feature that can be seen in the distance. Whilst at the walled circle, look over the quarry edge to the east for a good view of some quarrying machines that are set out below, superbly preserved from a bygone age. The area below is actually on the return path, but the route first continues north for 400m, keeping to the top of the ridge, before dropping down on to the track at SJ 94670 72940. There, turn back south, passing by the machines at the lower level.

The stone crusher, crane and swing saw are all preserved in their working state, with several information boards relating how they each played their part in the quarrying industry. The stone is Carboniferous limestone, laid down 350 million years ago when Britain was part of a landmass at the earth's equator. Although the quarry is now disused, in its day it produced huge amounts of paving and building materials. Indeed, it was said that Macclesfield was not paved with gold, but almost entirely with stone from Tegg's Nose quarry.

To leave Tegg's Nose, continue south along the track towards a point at SJ 94800 72310. On the way, you'll be able to appreciate the huge hole that has been excavated, but if you approach for a closer look, observe all the instructions shown on the various warning notices. At SJ 94800 72310, the route leads NE, down to a seat, then turns SE and zigzags its way down the hillside, emerging on to a farm track at the bottom. Turn left there, through a five-bar gate. Then follow the track on to and across the road-junction, continuing down the hill, past a farm and finally NE along the lane to SJ 95440 72750, where it becomes a stony track and turns SE.

After 400m, at SJ 95700 72430, the track turns sharp left (NE) and joins another lane at Hardingland. It's then only 150m to the stile on the right that leads to the path through the northern section of the forest. It's a well-walked path, but crossed by several others; do not be tempted to take any that drop down the hill into the depths of the forest. At one point, the path passes to the right of an old stone building, with a major crossroads of paths to the fore. Take the path directly opposite, over the stile, and continue on a steadily rising path for another 1km, finally emerging through a gate on to a walled track on the other side of the forest.

From there, the route home is straightforward. Walk 300m SE down the walled track (most of the time, it's also the route for a stream), go straight across the crossroads at the bottom (with a chapel on the left) and continue for another 400m SE to a T-junction. Turn right there, walking 400m south and then turning left (east) down the steep hill. At the bottom, turn right on to the Wildboarclough lane, stretching out your stride for the final 2.5km of road walking, the Clough Brook accompanying the route all the way back to the car.

Route summary

Your present location	Your next objective	Waypoint at next objective	Directions
Start, roadside pull-off SJ 98270 68730	Drive to right, marked 'Private' and 'Walkers Only'	SJ 98270 68680	300m SSW along the lane
SJ 98270 68680	Perimeter wall of Shutlingsloe Farm	SJ 98140 69300	700m along the steep drive
SJ 98140 69300	Shutlingsloe pillar	SJ 97645 69574	600m NW; a steep climb
SJ 97645 69574	Entrance to Macclesfield Forest	SJ 97170 70350	1.2km of paved path, walking NNW
SJ 97170 70350	Lane, with Trentabank Reservoir opposite	SJ 96260 71160	1.2km NW through the forest
SJ 96260 71160	Leather's Smithy public house	SJ 95250 71540	800m round north side of Ridgegate Reservoir
SJ 95250 71540	Entry into area of Bottoms Reservoir	SJ 94470 71550	800m west along the lane
SJ 94470 71550	Entrance to Tegg's Nose country park	SJ 94550 71830	300m NE and north, across the two dams
SJ 94550 71830	Top of the steep climb, at the gate for Tegg's Nose	SJ 94740 72300	800m climb, north and NE. Turn left at the gate
SJ 94740 72300	Second gate	SJ 94680 72480	200m north, then turn SE, then north before a third gate
SJ 94680 72480	Skylark's View information point	SJ 94770 72500	100m north, Blakelow Hill to west
SJ 94770 72500	Stone viewing circle	SJ 94780 72680	80m north
SJ 94780 72680	Track, to turn back	SJ 94670 72940	300m NNW, then turn back SE on the track
SJ 94670 72940	Path to descend from Tegg's Nose	SJ 94800 72310	800m south, past the machines and quarry
SJ 94800 72310	Farm track at bottom	SJ 95110 72580	500m generally NE, zigzagging down the hill
SJ 95110 72580	Right turn at end of lane, on to a stone track	SJ 95440 72750	300m NE, across road junction and past a farm
SJ 95440 72750	Left turn, where stone track veers NE	SJ 95700 72430	400m SE on the track
SJ 95700 72430	Forest entry	SJ 95950 72540	300m, NE on the track, then east on the lane
SJ 95950 72540	Forest exit	SJ 97170 72270	1.2km ESE through the forest
SJ 97170 72270	Cross-roads by chapel	SJ 97410 72110	300m SE
SJ 97410 72110	T-junction	SJ 97760 71840	450m SE, turn right
SJ 97760 71840	T-junction	SJ 97790 71450	400m south, turn left
SJ 97790 71450	T-junction	SJ 98220 71360	450m east, turn right
SJ 98220 71360	Car pull-off area	SJ 98270 68730	2.5km south to the car

Walk 19 – The Roaches and Gun

Start: Roadside pull-off, under Hen Cloud, opposite the drive west to Windygates – Map Reference SK 00610 61610

Distance: 17.5km (11 miles)

Total ascent: 570m (1830 ft)

Estimated time: 5.5 hours

Grading: Moderate

OS map: Explorer map OL 24 The Peak District – White Peak area

The route

The route follows the Roaches ridge path to the pillar, drops down through Back Forest and Lud's Church cave, passing Swythamley Hall on the way to the Gun pillar. The return is via the pastureland of Stockmeadows and Pheasant's Clough.

The height profile shows two significant climbs, so that the total ascent is 570m. Both pillars are on their local highest points.

The walk

From the pull-off area, proceed northwards along the lane to a stile set in the wall at SK 00620 61890, leading on to the Roaches Estate. To the immediate east is 'Hen Cloud', with its dramatic rock faces. Like other areas along the Roaches, it's very popular with climbers, with many difficult challenges for the enthusiasts. From the stile, follow the path NE for 150m, turning north through a wall gate and beginning the ascent to the Roach End ridge. It's only a moderately steep incline, but can be a slippery scramble if the conditions are wet.

The best approach to the ridge is to follow the path NNW along the top of the wooded area on the west side, with the high rock cliffs (and likely climbers) to the east. At SK 00510 62470 there is a set of steps (eastwards) leading up to the summit. There, cloud permitting, outstanding views of the surrounding Cheshire and Staffordshire countryside expand behind. To the SW is TittesworthReservoir, often mirrored against the dark green countryside by the morning sun. To the west is Gun Hill, where the second pillar on this walk is situated. To the east are the Ramshaw Rocks, another popular climbing area.

Once on the top, walk NNW, following the ridge for 400m up to 'Doxey Pool' at SK 00370 62850. It is supposedly bottomless, with a resident mermaid, both myths of course! But it is an unusual feature in that it remains full all the year round, even though it appears to have a very small rainwater catchment area.

From the pool to the pillar is 1.1km, following the ridge through the many fascinating gritstone rock formations. On the way, the path passes close to an old

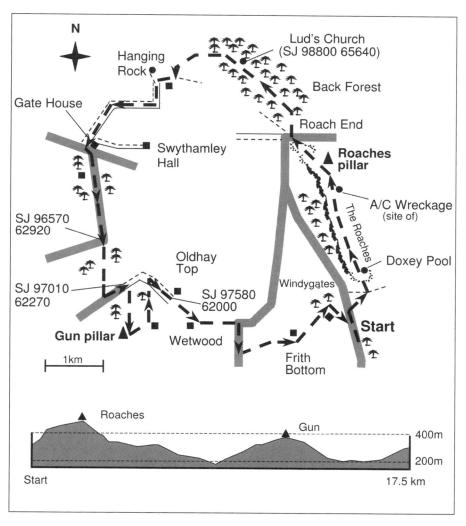

aircraft crash site; an Avro Lancaster bomber that came down in January 1945 whilst on a training flight from Waddington. The site is at SK 00150 63620, about 20m off the path, but is now no more than an area of peat exposed amongst the heather, with just a few fragments of melted metal and some small memorial crosses.

The Roaches pillar is mounted on a rough outcrop of rocks overlooking the Meerbrook valley to the west. It remains in reasonable condition, but with the original OS plug being replaced by a plastic insert.

The pillar details are:

Position: SK 00107 63891
Flush bracket No: S2598
Height: 506m (1645 ft)
Horizon: 80km (50 miles)
Built: June 1939
Historic use: Secondary
Current use: None
Condition: Fair

The Roaches pillar

The pillar triangulates with about 15 others, mostly to the south and west. Croker Hill, with its BT tower, The Cloud and Shutlingsloe are all unmistakable, and even Mow Cop, with its distinctive castle folly, is visible at a distance of 16km. The closest pillar, to the SW, is Gun, but the second closest pillar at Tittesworth Farm (5.5km south) is not visible, being just obscured by the Roaches ridge itself.

After the pillar, the path continues NW for 800m, descending to a lane at Roach End (SJ 99540 64460). Cross the lane, passing through a stile in the stone wall opposite, immediately turning right (north) over another stile. The path then follows the wall northwards for 300m before

Pillar	Distance	Direction
Axe Edge	7.5km	NNE (026 deg)
Blake Mere (Primary)	10.9km	SESE (125 deg)
Bradnop	10.3km	SSE (158 deg)
Moor Top	9.0km	SSE (161 deg)
Kniveden Reservoir *	7.8km	S (181 deg)
Hilly Field	6.4km	SSW (200 deg)
Dunwood	10.1km	WSSW (209 deg)
Brown Edge	13.4km	SW (223 deg)
Gun	3.9km	SWSW (232 deg)
High Bent	9.6km	WSW (241 deg)
Mow Cop	15.6km	WSW (246 deg)
The Cloud	9.6km	W (268 deg)
Croker Hill *	7.7km	NWNE (300 deg)
Shutlingsloe	6.2km	NNW (336 deg)
Shining Tor **	9.9km	N (355 deg)

* Pillars destroyed ** The visibility to Shining Tor is marginal

turning NW and leading down into Back Forest. The last section of the path is very rocky, and particularly hard on the feet. Upon entering the southern most end of Back Forest, follow the finger post for Danebridge. The paths NW through the wooded area are easy to follow, but much of the ground is criss-crossed by exposed tree roots. They can be very slippery if trodden on.

The forest itself is well known for its sightings of Australian wallabies, the animals having first appeared on the Roaches during the Second World War. A Col. Brocklehurst, the owner of the nearby Swythamley Hall at the time, started a private zoo on his estate after his return from Sudan. But during the Second World War, when food became scarce, the animals were released into the coun-tryside. The wallabies survived and bred around the Roaches for at least 50

Doxey Pool

years, and sightings have surprised many walkers and climbers. The last sighting by the authors was in 2002, near the southern entrance to Lud's Church.

Continue following the forest path for 1km, generally NW, looking out for the next finger post, indicating 'Lud's Church'. The first entrance to the cave is marked as being dangerous and is to be avoided. The entrance proper (at SJ 98800 65640) is a short distance further on, the stone steps worn smooth by thousands of walkers. Lud's Church is a cleft, rather than a closed cave, where a land slip within the underlying shale rocks has detached a large section of gritstone from the hillside, forming a gorge some 15m deep, 100m long, and two or three metres wide. It's a natural refuge, and throughout the ages the area has offered a hiding place to many persecuted groups, some mythical perhaps, but many factual.

One such story, the legend as told by Sir William de Lacey in 1546, is widely believed to be authentic. The gorge was used as a congregational area (hence the word 'church') by the followers of John Wycliffe, a church reformer of the 14th century. Known as 'Lollards' they were condemned as heretics, and one of their

A gallery within Lud's Church

most zealous supporters was a man called Walter de Lud-auk, himself an infamous Luddite. Consequently, the local ecclesiastical authorities sought every means possible to incriminate him.

At one meeting, whilst Walter de Lud-auk took the service, his eighteen-year-old grand-daughter Alice, a girl with a rare quality of voice, sang the hymn with such fervour that it resounded far beyond the secret church. It was then that an armour-clad troop burst in, the soldiers challenging the congregation in the name of King Henry. In the confrontation that followed, a shot was fired, aimed at a forester who openly resisted, the bullet missing its target and killing the luckless girl. Legend now has it that Alice is buried close to the cave, her spirit perhaps adding to the strange claustrophobic atmosphere that some walkers experience as they negotiate the gorge.

Leaving Lud's Church at the northern exit, continue NW along the path. After 500m, it emerges from the forest and turns west. At the next finger post (at SJ 97720 65510, 800m from the forest), follow the direction for Danebridge, then turn SW at the next post, this time towards Swythamley. The path drops down to a four-way junction (SJ 97420 65290), immediately below the 'Hanging Stone' rock to the north. Here again there is evidence of Col. Brocklehurst's influence in the area, with his memorial plaque ('In memory of Lt. Col. Brocklehurst of Swythamley Hall, who was killed in action whilst serving in Burma during World War II') fixed to the stone. A path leads to the rock for those who wish to make the visit.

Taking the southern route from the junction, continue for 1.5km down a limestone drive, the route first leading south, then west, then south again, before reaching the Gatehouse entrance to Swythamley Hall. Turn right at the Gatehouse, then immediately left on to the lane, heading south. After 100m, take the right fork and follow the lane for 1.5km, before going off-road again at SJ 96570 62920 by entering the no-through road at Gun End Farm. This route continues through grassy fields, following a chain of stiles to a metalled drive, where the route veers NE for 500m before turning south at SJ 97010 62270 on to Gun Moor and up to the trig point.

Gun pillar is mounted on a pleasant grassy site, nicely preserved and maintained, and with all its original features intact, including the OS plug in the spider.

The pillar triangulates with about 15 others, again mostly to the south and west. Croker Hill is only just visible over Bosley Minn, but The Cloud, Shutlingsloe and Mow Cop are all in clear view. The closest pillar, to the NE, is The Roaches, and now the pillar at Tittesworth Farm can be seen, with the view no longer blocked by The Roaches ridge.

The pillar details are:

Position: SJ 97006 61515
Flush bracket No: S2615
Height: 386m (1255 ft)
Horizon: 70km (44 miles)
Built: June 1939
Historic use: Secondary
Current use: None
Condition: Good

Gun pillar

The site has an interesting history. In the 1800s, it was used as a place of execution, the gibbet finally being removed in 1860. But that was not before a certain John Naden was convicted and hanged for murder, after he'd had an affair with his employer's wife and she'd urged him to kill her husband. When the gibbet was dismantled, the wood was reused to build stiles in the Bosley area, and sightings of the ghost of John Naden have been reported at several of these sites. The suggestion is that he is not a friendly spirit to meet!

Pillar	Distance	Direction
Shutlingsloe	8.1km	N (004 deg)
Shining Tor	12.5km	NNNE (011 deg)
The Roaches	3.9km	NENE (052 deg)
Blake Mere (Primary)	7.1km	E (094 deg)
Tittesworth Farm	4.7km	SE (133 deg)
Moor Top	8.6km	SE (136 deg)
Kniveden Reservoir *	6.2km	ESSE (151 deg)
Dunwood	6.6km	SSW (196 deg)
The Common	4.7km	SSW (200 deg)
Brown Edge	9.6km	SW (220 deg)
High Bent	5.8km	WSW (247 deg)
Mow Cop	11.8km	WSW (250 deg)
The Cloud	6.9km	WNW (288 deg)
Tidnock	12.0km	NWNW (305 deg)
Croker Hill *	7.7km	NWNE (300 deg)

* Pillars destroyed

From the pillar, follow the narrow path down through the heather in a NE direction. The lower section is sometimes vague, but the point to head for is the stile in front of the small-holding immediately below. Over the stile, turn left on to a grass track, walking north for 300m on to a concrete drive, then turn NE on to the limestone drive that leads to Oldhay Top. 200m before the farm, at SJ 97580 62000, take the stile on the right of the drive into the fields and then follow the chain of stiles to Wetwood Farm. It's 600m in a SE direction, crossing a stream over a wooden bridge near the farm. Progressing through the north side of the farmyard, take the drive that goes due east, meeting the lane at SJ 98800 61720.

Follow the lane south for 500m and then, at SJ 98780 61220, turn NNE along the drive to Frith Bottom. Just before entering the farmyard at Frith Bottom, cross to the stile on the right of the drive. It takes the path over several pontoons, then to another stile, before entering fields again. Head NE for 200m, picking up the next finger post at SJ 99520 61420. There, turn ESE to a stile at SJ 99770 61260, where the path turns once more and heads NW through Windygates Farm. The path leads to the left of the farm buildings, where it joins the farm drive leading back to the lane and the starting point.

Route summary

Your present location	Your next objective	Waypoint at next objective	Directions
Start, Hen Cloud SK 00610 61610	Stile in wall to east side of lane	SK 00620 61890	300m north along the lane
SK 00620 61890	Turning left, towards wall gate 150m to north	SK 00740 61980	150m NE from lane
SK 00740 61980	Set of stone steps, leading east to the top	SK 00510 62470	600m NNE, climbing to the west of the cliff side
SK 00510 62470	Doxey Pool	SK 00370 62850	400m NNW
SK 00370 62850	Point just east of the Lancaster aircraft wreckage	SK 00120 63620 (Wreckage is at SK 00150 63620)	850m from the pool, walking first NNW, then north
SK 00120 63620	Roaches pillar	SK 00107 63891	250m north
SK 00107 63891	Roach End	SJ 99540 64460	800m NW, downhill
SJ 99540 64460	Enter Back Forest	SJ 99470 64940	400m north and NW; rough rocky path at end
SJ 99470 64940	Lud's Church	SJ 98800 65640	1.2km NW in the forest
SJ 98800 65640	Exit the forest	SK 98420 65800	500m WNW from Lud's exit
SK 98420 65800	Finger post by gate	SJ 97720 65510	800m, first W, then SW
SJ 97720 65510	Junction of drives below Hanging Stone	SJ 97420 65290	Go south, then SW, then west. 500m total
SJ 97420 65290	Gate House	SJ 96410 64580	1.5km along the limestone drive,
SJ 96410 64580	Right fork in the lane, where the route turns right	SJ 96370 64530	Go right at the Gatehouse, left on the lane, and on to the right fork
SJ 96370 64530	Drive, by Gun End Farm	SJ 96570 62920	1.5km SSE on the lane
SJ 96570 62920	Metalled drive	SJ 96560 62000	1km south, turn NE
SJ 96560 62000	Stile and path to Gun	SJ 97010 62270	500m NE up the drive
SJ 97010 62270	Gun pillar	SJ 97006 61515	750m south
SJ 97006 61515	Stile, NE of pillar	SJ 97210 61730	300m through heather
SJ 97210 61730	Right turn from the drive	SJ 97190 62060	350m north, turn right
SJ 97190 62060	Stile, Oldhay Top	SJ 97580 62000	350m east, enter fields
SJ 97580 62000	Wetwood Farm	SJ 98070 61700	600m SE, take first drive east
SJ 98070 61700	Lane, go right there	SJ 98800 61720	750m along the drive
SJ 98800 61720	Drive to Frith Bottom	SJ 98780 61220	500m south down lane
SJ 98780 61220	Frith Bottom Farm, where the route goes anticlockwise around it	SJ 99320 61340	600m east. To go round the farm, take the stile south, over pontoons. Then, after 100m, turn NE
SJ 99320 61340	Finger Post	SJ 99520 61420	250m NE from Frith Bottom Farm
SJ 99520 61420	Stile	SJ 99770 61260	300m, SE of the post
SJ 99770 61260	Back to start	SK 00610 61610	1.2km NE, then East, past Windygates

Walk 20 – Blake Mere, Revidge and Hill House

Start: At the 'Mermaid' viewpoint, on the lane overlooking The Roaches from the east, 6km NE of Leek – Map reference SK 02860 59610

Distance: 14.8km (9.3 miles)

Total ascent: 410m (1320 ft)

Estimated time: 5 hours

Grading: Moderate

OS map: Explorer map OL 24 The Peak District – White Peak area

The route

The route takes in Merryton Low, visiting the Blake Mere pillar, uses the lanes to reach the Revidge summit, then continues to the Hill House pillar via open pastures around Upper Elkstone. The final leg is along good tracks across High Moor.

The profile shows the walk starting at a high point, with relatively gentle gradients until the approach to Hill House, which is a demanding climb.

The walk

Before leaving the lay-by, take a minute to admire the panoramic scenery to the NW, with excellent views across Ramshaw Rocks and the Roaches (Walk 19), both very popular climbing venues. 11km distant, on the horizon to the right of Roach End, is the distinctive profile of Shutlingsloe, visited during Walk 18.

View of the Roaches

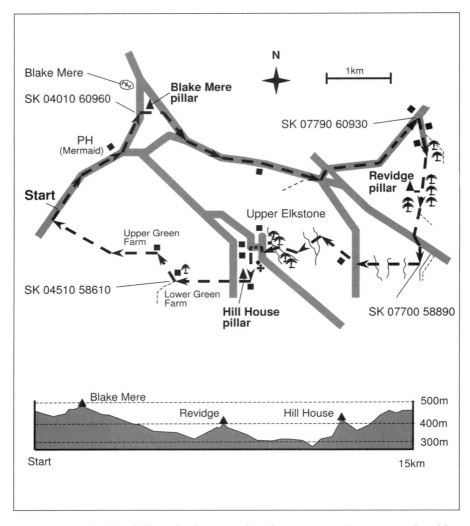

From the lay-by, follow the lane NE for 2km, passing the Mermaid public house and the lane opposite, up to a path leaving off to the right, marked 'Out of bounds to all MOD vehicles' (at SK 04010 60960). The reference to MOD vehicles marks the area as having been used for military training in the past, with other military restriction notices cropping up several times throughout the walk. Now, however, most of the area is Open Access.

The track leads directly to the first pillar, named Blake Mere, although it's actually situated on a hill called Merryton Low. Blake Mere itself is a very modest little pool, situated just to the west of the road junction 300m NNW of the pillar. Small as it is, legend says it boasts its own mermaid (hence the name of the nearby pub), but she is not to be trifled with, luring unsuspecting travellers and trigpointers to a watery grave!

The Blake Mere pillar is a Primary, and was one of the first dozen to be built, in early 1936. It remains in good condition, although the OS insert has been lost, replaced by a plastic plug. The site is a Passive Station, declared by a plaque attached to the pillar. It was last surveyed in September 1999 (the date on the plaque), when the height was measured as 488.901m. Also attached to the pillar is a plaque commemorating the members of the Staffordshire Regiment Home Guard who gave their lives during the Second World War.

Blake Mere pillar

The pillar details are:

Position: SK 04134 60999
Flush bracket No: 2989
Height: 489m (1589ft)
Horizon: 79km (49 miles)
Built: March 1936
Historic use: Primary
Current use: Passive Station
Condition: Good

Visibility to other pillars from the Blake Mere Primary is exceptional, with at least 36 in view within a 16km (10 mile) radius, all around the

Pillar	Distance	Direction
Hollinsclough Moor	5.0km	NNNE (016 deg)
Hind Low *	8.9km	NNE (026 deg)
High Wheeldon	7.8km	NE (049 deg)
Sheen Hill	7.1km	EENE (077 deg)
Bank Top	7.7km	EESE (097 deg)
Wolfscote Hill	9.9km	EESE (105 deg)
Revidge	3.8km	ESE(107 deg)
Ecton Hill	6.6km	ESE (017 deg)
Wetton Low	9.4km	SE (131 deg)
Soles Hill	10.2km	ESSE (146 deg)
Grindon Moor	6.6km	SSE (152 deg)
Hill House	2.7km	SSE (156 deg)
Bradnop	6.7km	S (182 deg)
Hilly Field	7.1km	WSW (243 deg)
The Common	9.6km	WSW (246 deg)
Gun	7.1km	W (273 deg)
The Roaches	4.9km	NWNW (305 deg)
Shutlingsloe	10.7km	WNNW (322 deg)
Axe Edge	9.6km	N (356 deg)

* Pillar missing

compass. It's probably one of the best Primary pillar sites in the country. To be practical, the table shows only those within 10km, but including Shutlingsloe (10.7km distant) because its profile in the NW is so distinctive. Curiously, one local pillar that is only 4.5km distant, Tittesworth Farm, is not in view, so that the value of that particular pillar site is in question.

As well as the local pillars, Blake Mere has line-of-sight to five Primary pillars in the Peak District. To the west, about 50km distant, there is also line-of-sight to the Wirswall and Delamere Primaries in square SJ, but perhaps they are too far off for triangulation.

Continuing on from the pillar, follow the path 160m east to a lane. Turn south, following the lane as it is joined by another from the right, then continuing generally SE, via Upper Hay Corner, for 3km to a road junction at SK 06770 59930. On the way, there are more signs warning of military access restrictions. Turn left at the road junction, going straight on at the next cross-roads (after 150m) and continuing NE along the lane for a further 1.3km to a right turn at SK 07790 60930. Before that, 600m from the cross-roads, the lane passes a point at SK 07300 60240 where the Revidge pillar is only 530m SE (bearing 127 deg) across the Open Access moor. It's usually wet, it's hard work, there's no path, but there are no barriers either.

However, our official route uses the lanes, turning right at the road junction at SK 07790 60930, heading SSE and rising towards Revidge Hill. After 450m, the lane reaches a gate and cattle grid at SK 07890 60450, marking the boundary of Open Access land. Take the right of the two tracks that leave from the gate, walking south amongst the trees up to a point where a log barrier bars the way. It's marked by a sign saying 'No MOD Vehicles beyond this point', further testimony to the military history of the area.

A path to the right of the barrier leads through a small wooded area up to the Revidge pillar, 150m to the west. The pillar is in good condition, painted white, with a stone plug replacing the OS insert, and accompanied by a curious stone dog sculpture, no doubt courtesy of a walker with an artistic flair.

The pillar details are:

Position: SK 07739 59910
Flush bracket No: S4171
Height: 400m (1300ft)
Horizon: 72km (45 miles)
Built: August 1947
Historic use: Secondary
Current use: None
Condition: Good

Revidge pillar, with sculpture

Visibility from Revidge is excellent, with 28 pillars in sight to a distance of 16km (10 miles). The table lists the closest 20, distributed all round the compass.

From the pillar, return east to the limestone track, following it south for 500m to a gate at SK 07820 59360. From the other side of the gate, the path across the field leads SSW for 200m, emerging onto a lane via a wall stile. Go left for 50m, crossing to the field path on the other side of the lane via a further wall stile. Follow the grass path SSW for 250m to a point where a drive approaches near to the path on the left (SK 07700 58890), turning right at that point and walking due west. The path is not very clear, but two old stone gateposts mark the direction the route follows, passing by a row of gorse bushes. From there, the path runs due west for 800m, first crossing a stream via a stile, a very slippery bridge and a set of rotting wooden steps, then negotiating two smaller streams before reaching a stile on to the lane at SK 06940 58870.

Turn north, walking 150m to a further stile on the west side of the lane and following the path NW across

Pillar	Distance	Direction
Hind Low *	9.1km	N (002 deg)
High Wheeldon	6.6km	NNE (020 deg)
Sheen Hill	4.2km	NENE (051 deg)
Parsley Hay Farm	8.1km	NENE (057 deg)
Lean Low	7.6km	ENE (072 deg)
Bank Top	4.1km	E (088 deg)
Aleck Low	9.8km	E (092 deg)
Wolfscote Hill	6.2km	EESE (104 deg)
Hawkes Low	9.6km	ESE (107 deg)
Ecton Hill	2.9km	SE (130 deg)
Reynards	10.3km	SE (134 deg)
Wetton Low	6.2km	ESSE (145 deg)
Soles Hill	8.4km	SSSE (164 deg)
Grindon Moor	4.8km	SSSW (186 deg)
Bradnop	6.8km	WSSW (214 deg)
Moor Top	6.6km	SW (226 deg)
Hill House	2.9km	WSW (242 deg)
Blake Mere (Primary)	3.7km	WWNW (286 deg)
Hollinsclough Moor	6.3km	NNW (339 deg)
Hardings Booth	4.1km	NNNW (353 deg)

* Pillar missing

open pastures, passing about 20m to the right of a ruined stone hut. After 400m, at SK 06520 59240, the path crosses a stream and joins a limestone drive through a gate, heading WSW. 350m onwards from the stream, at SK 06240 59100, with the drive then continuing SW, off the route towards Townhead, turn right over a stile to the right of a gate. From there, follow the track through the hollow, then take the field path westwards for 250m, reaching another stile at the edge of a wooded area (SK 05990 59120). The route turns NW, descending a steep and hazardous path through the wood, before turning SW to cross a stream via two bridges. On the other side it emerges on to open pasture, to the NE of Upper Elkstone. Take the stile in the top left (SW) corner of the field, following an alleyway out to the lane at Upper Elkstone (SK 05630 59030).

Turn right, following the lane towards Hob Hay for 100m as it loops round to the left, from NW round to SW. As the lane to Hob Hay turns sharp right, enter 'Well Lane' to the left, following it south to a fork, a tarmac drive then continuing right towards Hill House Farm. But keep to the limestone drive on the left, via a stile and gate, following it south for 300m towards a farm. 70m before the farm, take the stile on the right, immediately after passing though a gate. There is then a very steep 1 in 3 climb up the grass path to the Hill House pillar, crossing two more stiles on the way.

The base of the pillar has been exposed by erosion, but otherwise it remains in good condition. There is no OS insert, just a stone plug.

The pillar details are:

Position: SK 05169 58571
Flush bracket No: S4170
Height: 425m (1381ft)
Horizon: 74km (46 miles)
Built: August 1947
Historic use: Secondary
Current use: None
Condition: Fair

Hill House pillar

At least 24 local pillars can be seen within a distance of 16km (10 miles), but mostly in the eastern half of the compass. Views westwards are limited by the close proximity of High Moor, which is some 40m higher than the Hill House position. The table lists the 20 closest pillars, omitting three (Bank Top, The Roaches and Axe Edge) which have very marginal line-of-sight.

From the pillar, the route continues west, 100m down to a lane. Cross it, taking the stile immediately opposite and following the field path alongside a farm drive down to Lower Green Farm. There, the path joins the farm drive, the way onwards being over a stile set into the embankment on the right (SK 04510 58610). The route then passes through the farm, emerging alongside the right-hand fence (north) of a

Pillar	Distance	Direction
Hind Low *	10.8km	NNNE (016 deg)
High Wheeldon	9.0km	ENNE (032 deg)
Sheen Hill	7.1km	NENE (055 deg)
Parsley Hay Farm	11.0km	NENE (058 deg)
Revidge	2.9km	ENE (062 deg)
Lean Low	10.4km	ENE (069 deg)
Aleck Low	12.3km	E (085 deg)
Wolfscote Hill	8.5km	E (091 deg)
Ecton Hill	4.8km	EESE (097 deg)
Hawkes Low	12.2km	EESE (097 deg)
Reynards	11.5km	SESE (120 deg)
Wetton Low	7.3km	SESE (122 deg)
Musden Low	10.8km	ESSE (141 deg)
Soles Hill	7.6km	ESSE (142 deg)
Grindon Moor	4.0km	SSE (150 deg)
Hoftens Cross	11.1km	SSSE (167 deg)
Black Heath	8.7km	S (181 deg)
Bradnop	4.5km	SSW (197 deg)
Moor Top	3.9km	WSSW (214 deg)
Blake Mere (Primary)	2.6km	NNW (337 deg)

* Pillar missing

paddock area, there picking up a well-signposted grass path leading on to Upper Green Farm. The route again passes amongst the farm buildings, exiting on to a limestone drive, which defines the route WNW for the final 1.5km back to the lane and the Mermaid viewpoint.

Route summary

Your present location	Your next objective	Waypoint at next objective	Directions
Start, Mermaid Viewpoint SK 02860 59610	Track leaving to right, marked 'No MOD Vehicles'	SK 04010 60960	2km NE along the lane, passing the 'Mermaid' PH
SK 04010 60960	Blake Mere pillar	SK 04134 60999	120m east
SK 04134 60999	Junction of lanes	SK 06770 59930	160m east to lane, then 3km SE
SK 06770 59930	Turning right down lane	SK 07790 60930	1.3km NE on lane
SK 07790 60930	Cattle grid and gate, Open Access land	SK 07890 60450	450m south on lane
SK 07890 60450	Log barrier	SK 07900 59920	500m south on track
SK 07900 59920	Revidge pillar	SK 07739 59910	150m west on path
SK 07739 59910	Log barrier	SK 07900 59920	150m east on path
SK 07900 59920	Gate	SK 07820 59360	500m south on track
SK 07820 59360	Stile on to lane	SK 07780 59180	200m SSW on field path.
SK 07780 59180	Point to turn right on grass path, where a track is close by to left	SK 07700 58890	On lane, go 50m south to the stile opposite. Then 250m SSW on grass path
SK 07700 58890	Stile to lane	SK 06940 58870	800m west over three streams
SK 06940 58870	Stile, west side of lane	SK 06880 59030	150m north on lane
SK 06880 59030	Stream crossing, on to limestone track	SK 06520 59240	400m NW on grass path
SK 06520 59240	Stile and gate, to NW	SK 06240 59100	350m SW on track
SK 06240 59100	Stile to wood	SK 05990 59120	250m west, track and then grass path
SK 05990 59120	Stile to alleyway and lane, Upper Elkstone	SK 05630 59030	300m total, through wood and across field
SK 05630 59030	Well Lane	SK 05550 59060	100m on lane, looping NW to SW
SK 05550 59060	Stile after gate, on right	SK 05520 58560	450m south on drive and farm track
SK 05520 58560	Hill House pillar	SK 05169 58571	350m west on very steep grass path
SK 05169 58571	Stile to route through Lower Green Farm	SK 04510 58610	West to lane, cross it, grass path to farm, 700m total
SK 04510 58610	Upper Green Farm	SK 04260 58970	450m NW, by paddock, then grass path
SK 04260 58970	Mermaid Viewpoint	SK 02860 59610	1.5km NNW on track, to lane, turn right to car

Access to other Peak District pillars

In this and the following section on drive-by visits, we discuss the remaining peak district pillars, listed north to south. There is information on how best to reach them, group them into practical walks and, if they are on private land, where to ask permission for access, if known. If there is a reasonable walk, either to a single pillar or to a group of two or three, it is given an identification letter as shown in the 'The Walks' section, with the geographical location map. Those pillars that are visited as a 'drive-by', with just a short distance to the site, are not included in such walks. The pillar coordinates can be found in the Introduction (Table 2), and please refer to the Explorer OL1 and OL24 Peak District maps when planning your visits.

Walks A to X

Walk A – Alphin Pike (SE 00296 02817)

For a moderate 14km walk, approach the pillar from Mossley, along 'White Gate', returning via Wimberry Moss ridge, Chew Brook and the Dovestones reservoir, all Open Access.

Walk B – Cobden Edge (SJ 98675 87249) and Marple Ridge (SJ 96215 87266)

Park in Mellor and plan an easy 11km walk that includes the footpaths around 'The Banks' and 'Strawberry Hill', crossing the River Goyt. The Marple Ridge pillar is within a housing estate, so ask one of the householders about access.

Walk C – Chinley Churn (SK 03549 83633)

Make a pleasant 8km walk from Chinley railway station by taking the lane NE to 'Peep o Day' and coming back west on the high ground above the edge. Cracken Edge is Open Access, but the pillar is on private land. It can be viewed from SK 03750 83500, 250m to the SE.

Walk D – Sir William Hill (SK 21538 77891) and Abney Moor (SK 18043 79421)

To bag these two pillars in one pleasant 15km walk, start in Eyam and walk north to the Sir William Hill pillar (Open Access) before continuing via Stanage, Highlow Brook, Smelting Hill and the north section of Abney Moor. Then use the track across Robin Hood's Cross to reach the Open Access area of Abney Moor south, viewing the pillar from SK 18160 79410.

Walk E – Nab Head (SJ 94007 78837), Kerridge Hill (SJ 94245 75948) and Sponds Hill (SJ 97001 80294)

A strenuous 17km round trip of these three pillars starts from Bollington. Take the lane towards Pott Shrigley and follow the concession path through a housing estate to the Nab Head summit, returning the same way. Then take the route along Kerridge Ridge, visiting the curious 'White Nancy' folly on the way to the Kerridge pillar. From there to Sponds Hill needs some planning, but there is a long section of the Gritstone Way which is pleasant walking. Finish the walk by returning via Dale Top and Pott Shrigley.

Walk F – Wheston (SK 13841 76565) and Wormhill (SK 10721 75621)

There is a moderate 16km circular walk to take in these two pillars, including the picturesque valley of Chee Dale and the Limestone Way. Wheston pillar is on private land, so ask locally about access. Wormhill pillar is on Bole Hill, NW of Tunstead. It's private, and it's important to ask permission at the farm to the north, at SK 10960 76360.

Walk G – Wardlow (SK 17851 73972) and High Rake (SK 20881 73402)

A pleasant 15km walk past these pillars is best from Great Longstone, along the ridges and back round the small reservoir to the north, on to Little Longstone. The High Rake pillar is badly damaged, within the bounds of the quarry. On a Sunday, the security patrolman might well escort you to the spot. The Wardlow pillar is on land owned by English Nature, with no obvious problem of access. There is a path out of Wardlow village, leading west, so that it's possible to walk south from that. But to complete the loop via Ravensdale and Cressbrook there is no way down the steep-sided valley other than by returning to that path to the north.

Walk H – Sough Top (SK 13330 70896)

We recommend a 13km walk along Wye Dale, Chee Dale and Miller's Dale, then south down the Limestone Way to visit the pillar. It's on private land, 100m off the footpath. A return leg via Churn Hole makes for a pleasant walk.

Walk I – Axe Edge (SK 03502 70613), taking in Grin Low Tower

Approach Axe Edge pillar from the lane to the SW, across the Open Access moor. Then you can make a reasonable 10km walk around the area by taking in the 'Solomon's Temple' tower on Grinlow Hill, 2km NE of Axe Edge. It has an Ordnance Survey bolt (SK 05431 71738) in the centre of the top floor. Continue via the Dane Valley Way, taking in the Buxton Country Park and Poole's Cavern and returning around the north, via Burbage.

Hitter, Parkhouse and Chrome Hills, north from High Wheeldon

Walk J – Hind Low (SK 08087 68960, missing) and High Wheeldon (SK 10037 66111)

High Wheeldon is a splendid pillar site on a prominent National Trust hill near Earl Sterndale, with superb views of the White Peak. The best approach is from the lane to the NE, with a marked footpath up to the summit. For a moderate 12km walk, continue via the dramatic limestone coral hills of Chrome Hill and Parkhouse Hill (both Open Access), round the top of Upper Edge, and finally skirt the Hind Low quarry to log the site of the missing pillar.

Walk K – High Low (SK 15571 67700) and Bole Hill (SK 18403 67589)

The approach to High Low is easy from the footpath to the NW, but the pillar is on private land so ask locally about access. Along with Bole Hill, the site is close to Lathkill Dale to the south, so that a pleasant 15km walk that takes in the valley and the two pillars is quite feasible, parking in Monyash. For Bole Hill, ask at Bole Hill Farm to the SE of the pillar.

Walk L – Noton Barn (SK 21667 66169) and Long Rake (SK 18363 64158)

These are two other visits that can be made via Lathkill Dale. Noton Barn pillar is within a few metres of a footpath, whereas Long Rake is on private land. It's important to ask permission at the farm to the west of the site. A 16km circular walk down the Long Rake lane and the dale passes the interesting henge at Arbor Low.

Arbor Low henge

Walk M – The Cloud (SJ 90469 63659)

Start at the Pool Bank car park (SJ 89200 63040) and plan an easy 7km route eastwards to the summit and then south down the lane on the east side to visit the 'Bridestones', a fascinating Megalithic burial chamber.

Walk N – Bank Top (SK 11802 60064), Lean Low (SK 14956 62235) and Sheen Hill (SK 11055 62539)

A starting point for a pleasant 15km walk round these three pillars is the picturesque village of Hartington. Walk the lane eastwards, cross the Tissington Trail and pick up a path that runs NNE towards Lean Low Farm. Ask there for access to the Lean Low pillar and take advice on how best to regain the Tissington Trail across the open pastures. Then walk to Parsley Hay and westwards via Pilsbury to the Sheen Hill pillar, approaching along the drive from the NNE and asking at the house near the trig point. From there, walk south through Sheen, turn left at Townend, following the drive down to Banktop Farm and asking there about access to Bank Top.

Walk O – Moor Plantations (SK 24496 62906), Hopping Top (SK 20977 62718) and Elton Common (SK 22069 60220)

For a 15km round trip, start at the Elton Common pillar and walk north through Elton village, following the footpath that skirts close to the Hopping Top pillar. Then head eastwards to take in Robin Hood's Stride rocks on the way to Birchover. The Moor Plantation pillar is to the NE of Birchover, on Stanton Moor, with several ancient features to visit, including the Nine Ladies stone circle. Moor Plantations is Open Access, but Hopping Top and Elton Common are on private land, the landowners uncertain, so enquire of a local before venturing off the rights of way.

Walk P – Ecton Hill (SK 09979 57998) and Wetton Low (SK 11223 54743)

These two pillars make a good pairing, with Wetton Mill, Wetton Hill and the Sugarloaf hill between them. Park in Ecton and take in the Ecton Hill pillar first. It's close to a path, on land that is well walked. From there, plan a walk taking in the National Trust area to the south, through Wetton village and out to the Wetton Low pillar. It's an easy walk up to that pillar from the lane that runs SE out of Wetton, but ask a local about where to seek permission. The return can be at lower level, via Wetton Mill, the valley lane and the tunnel at Swainsley.

Walk Q – Wolfscote Hill (SK 13705 58323)

Wolfscote Hill is National Trust, with access from the south. For a pleasant 11km walk, start in Hartington, going SE and then south down Biggin Dale, returning along Wolfscote Dale to the north end, and visiting the pillar on a 'there and back' detour via Wolfscote Grange. The return is along Beresford Dale.

Walk R – Aleck Low (SK 17502 59475), and Hawks Low (SK 16972 57028)

Park in Gotham, walk NW on the Midshires Way and ask at Upperhouse Farm for Aleck Low. From that pillar, it's possible to walk west and then south down the Tissington Trail. But to make a loop that brings in Hawks Low is not easy, since it's necessary to ask at Hawkslow Farm. Once visited, the route back from the pillar to Gotham is straightforward, making the trip 17km.

Walk S – Dunwood (SJ 95148 55116), Hilly Field (SJ 97819 57877) and The Common (SJ 95344 57128)

It's possible to make a reasonable 15km walk around these three pillars. Park in Abbey Green and plan a walk that uses the lanes and the pleasant section of the Staffordshire Way along the river at Longsdon. The Hilly Field pillar in Abbey Green is by a lane off the A523 out of Leek. The site is in a horse paddock, so ask at the farm and stables 100m across the road to the south of the pillar.

For The Common, walk up the drive to Harracles Hall (just south of Rudyard) and ask permission. The pillar is 100m to the south of the drive. Finally, Dunwood is an oddity. It's buried deep in a hedge, 50m into a field by the side of a lane, so in summer it may be very difficult to find, even with the GPS. Access is best from Longsdon on the A53, but the landowner is uncertain, so be prepared to make a local enquiry.

Walk T – Slipper Low (SK 22701 56897), Blackstones Low (SK 21000 55420) and Harborough Rocks (SK 24264 55337)

These three pillars can be grouped in a pleasant 14km walk from Grangemill, making use of the Limestone Way, the Midshires Way and the lanes around Longcliffe. Slipper Low is on private land, but only 200m from the lane. Ask per-

The pillar's namesake, Reynards Cave, Dove Dale

mission at Green Farm to the north. Blackstones Low is Open Access land and is best approached from the west, using the metalled road that goes on to Royston Grange. It's advisable to plan a route using the Limestone Way to the south of the pillar. Finally, Harborough Rocks is public access, positioned on some interesting limestone rock formations.

Walk U – Reynards (SK 15107 52677)

Reynards pillar stands on the high ground to the east of the spectacular Dove Dale valley, and it fits well into a 14km walk northwards along the River Dove, starting from the southern end. Leave the north end at Milldale, returning SE and south using the footpath that passes Bostern Grange Farm. Enquire there about the best way to approach the pillar.

Return must be back to the path and then on to the lane to the east, with options around Thorp Pastures and Lin Dale to complete the loop. Walking westwards from the pillar in the hope of dropping back down into Dove Dale is not advisable.

Walk V – Soles Hill (SK 09794 52505) and Musden Low (SK 11832 50080)

The area around Waterfall and the Hamps valley provides pleasant walking, and it's easy to make a 15km circuit of these two pillars. Soles Hill is on open pastureland to the east of the National Trust area along the River Hamps. It's best approached from the public footpath that runs to the east of the pillar, then returning to that path to continue the circuit. It is private land, so ask for permission at the farm located 500m SE of the pillar.

Musden Low is also private, but a very popular walking area with many paths and stiles. It's a pleasant pasture summit with no obvious problems of access.

Walk W – Wibben Hill (SK 18374 52247) and Madge Hill (SK 21863 49595)

A 13km walk round these two pillars can start in Tissington, first visiting Wibben Hill, then using the lanes and public footpaths to Kniverton. From there, the route is SE on footpaths to Madge Hill, down the green lane to Woodhead, and finally returning NW using the paths and lanes. Wibben Hill pillar is 50m off the public footpath and can be visited without intrusion. Madge Hill is 20m off the green lane, with a farm close by where a polite request can be made.

Walk X – Hoftens Cross (SK 07629 47766), Milk Hill (SK 09350 49560) and Weaver Hill (SK 09454 46389, Primary)

When walking the 12km between these three pillars, the best starting point is the parking area in Waterhouses, just off the A52 trunk road down the lane to Cauldon. Plot a route SW towards Milk Hill, asking about access at Middlehills Farm, then go south past The Dale and Weaver Farm. Use the path returning NW to visit the Weaver Hill pillar; it's off the official path, but is well frequented. It's a Primary, with superb views all round.

From Weaver Hill continue NW, skirting the north of the quarry near Wardlow, and visit the Hoftens Cross pillar (actually situated on Cauldon Low). It's private, but with no obvious clue to the landowner, so enquire of a local. Access from the lane is easy. From there, return north via the Caldon quarry area, but be prepared for changes in the rights of way.

Drive-by visits and single pillars requiring only a short walk

Standedge (SE 01236 10415)

Standedge pillar is a 1km walk NW along the Pennine Way from the car park next to Brunsclough, at SE 01850 09470. It's in poor condition, having been extensively repaired.

West Nab (SE 07644 08792)

Park on the lane that passes below West Nab, at SE 01890 08980, and follow the track 400m to the pillar. Unfortunately, the 'Rocking Stone' nearby has been pushed off its plinth by vandals, having rocked there since the Ice Age.

West Nab pillar - the rocking stone to the right tipped from its plinth

Saddleworth (SE 02076 06964)

This is best approached from the A635, parking on a pull-off at SE 02280 05930. Make the stiff climb to the fence at the top and then follow it round to the east and north before striking off across the Open Access moor. The pillar is in poor condition, having been vandalised, but repaired by a local walking club.

Whitwell Moor (SK 24972 97237)

The pillar is in a popular Open Access walking area, just north of the Broomhead reservoir, with pleasant views. Park in Bolterstone and walk 2km west to the pillar.

Ringinglow (SK 29957 83652)

Ask at Firs Farm, at SK 29550 83740. There is a path from there that leads south to the area of the pillar, but the site itself is on private land. It is best collected as a drive-by, along with the Blacka Plantation and Totley pillars (below).

Blacka Plantation (SK 28995 81251)

This is on private land. Approach from the north, having asked at the farm situated at SK 29100 81470. The path through the wood from the main road is not recommended.

Totley (SK 30344 79652)

Access is easy from the main road, 100m up to the top of a modest hill, behind a phone mast. The landowner is uncertain, so be prepared to make a local enquiry.

Bradwell Moor (SK 13179 80133)

The pillar is near the Limestone Way, on Open Access land. If approaching from Castleton, start at Cavedale, but the paths tend to be used by scrambler bikes. An alternative is from Peak Forest on the A623; then it's also possible to visit the Bee Low quarry site (below).

Bee Low (SK 09244 79147, missing)

This pillar fell victim to the Dove Holes quarry in 1966, and the flush bracket (S4227) was reused for the Jodrell Bank pillar. To log the site, follow the rights of way out of Doveholes, first taking a look at the Bull Ring henge, and skirt around the north of the quarry. The footpaths may change from those shown on OS maps, according to the quarry workings, but there are information boards explaining the new rights of way.

Ladder Hill (SK 02772 78867)

The pillar is on private land, close to a communication mast. Approach it from the east, first having enquired about access at Spire Hollins Farm in Thorney Lee.

Fairfield (SK 07770 74422)

This is easy to reach from a public footpath. But it's private, and it's necessary to ask at Daisymeer Farm just to the east of the pillar.

Birchen Edge (SK 27825 73093)

Birchen Edge has some splendid views, but the walk has to be a 'there and back' trip along the top, starting by the Robin Hood public house on the lane off the A619. On the way is Nelson's Monument, a rather plain obelisk, and close by are three rocks, vaguely ship-like in appearance, each carved with the name of a British fighting vessel.

Grange Hill (SK 31539 73609)

Drive east for 4km from Birchen Edge along the B6050; you'll come across the pillar at the side of the road.

Blakelow (SJ 93420 72395)

Strictly, this is Higher Blakelow. It's 1km to the west of Tegg's Nose, so you might make a visit after completing Walk 18 (Shutlinsloe). The best approach is via the lane and farm track to the north of the hill, but first ask permission at Higher Blakelow farm.

Calton Pastures (SK 23779 68174)

The pillar is in a pleasant location, with good views over the Chatsworth Estate. Park in Rowsley; it's then an easy walk NW through Manners Wood. But leave the wood on the mapped public footpath to the north and pick up the field path that runs SE-NW, 200m north of the pillar. Unobtrusive access is then straight-forward.

Harland South (SK 30088 68157, Primary and a Passive Station)

The pillar is only 100m from the road, clearly visible on Open Access land, and with excellent all round views. But entry to the heather moor must be through a gate off the lane at SK 29460 67730, which leaves 800m of hard walking to reach the pillar. On the way, take a look at the ancient signpost at SK 29920 67970.

Croker Hill (SJ 93372 67696, missing)

This one is missing, knocked over when the BT tower was being con-structed. The Gritstone Trail passes by the tower, so it's easy to log a visit.

Hollinsclough Moor (SK 05531 65838)

This pillar is just 20m from the lane, with a lay-by and a right of way down the nearby green lane. Hardings Booth pillar, another drive-by, is nearby to the SE.

Fallinge (SK 27612 65478)

This is best as a drive-by, possibly with Calton Pastures and Harland

Ancient signpost near Harland South

South that are both nearby. Access is easy from the lane to the north, along the public footpath that runs SSE and across the Open Access heather moor.

Parsley Hay Farm (SK 14594 64229)

The pillar is close to the A515 roadside, with a public footpath 150m to the north, so the approach across the open pastureland is easy. But ask first at Moscar Farm, on the opposite side of the main road.

Hardings Booth (SK 07203 63937)

Ask permission at 'Hillend', up the track just to the NW of the pillar. The pillar itself is badly damaged, situated in open pastureland.

Farley (SK 30053 62072)

Farley is a real challenge. It's in the centre of a forestry plantation, where most of the woodland tracks are unmarked on the OS maps. However, it is within 50m of one of the tracks and there is entry through an access point off a lane at SK 29920 63480. It's then 1.4km to the pillar.

Oaker Hill (SK 27120 61303)

It's a brief, stiff climb up a concession path to this splendid site overlooking Matlock. Take the narrow lane up the hill opposite the church in Darley Bridge and look for the access gate and notice.

Blakelow Hill (SK 25454 59395)

Access looks easy along the green lanes that run south and west from Tearsal Farm. But they are not rights of way, and the pasture field with the pillar is not accessible from the end of those lanes. Ask advice at Bonsal Lane Farm rather than Tearsal Farm.

High Bent (SJ 91559 59319)

The pillar is close to the roadside, to the east of the lane that runs north out of Biddulph Moor village. For a closer inspection, ask advice at one of the houses across the road.

Masson Hill (SK 28603 58670, missing)

The best approach is from the lane that runs WSW from Matlock, parallel to the Limestone Way path. In fact, the pillar is missing (Flush Bracket No S1718), replaced by a surface block and bolt.

Tittesworth Farm (SK 00403 58328)

Ask at the farm itself, at SK 00330 58500, off the A53 trunk road. The pillar is in the field at the back. It's in an odd position, since it triangulates with only one or two others.

Mow Cop Folly

Mow Cop (SJ 85841 57540)

The Mow Cop pillar overlooks the curious 'Old Man of Mow' gritstone rock pillar. Across the lane to the south of the pillar is the distinctive castle folly, built in 1754 by local stonemasons for Randle Wilbraham, the tower acting as a summerhouse.

Kniveden Reservoir (SJ 99923 56069, missing)

This pillar is missing (Flush Bracket No S2656), lost when the reservoir was created. The site is an open field off a lane from the A523, near the Lowe Hill area. Walk east up the drive from the lane and ask at the farm.

Batemans Plantation (SK 26759 55587)

The pillar is on open farmland between areas of quarrying. The landowner is unknown, so enquire locally. There is easy walking from Middleton or from the lane to the south of the pillar.

Moor Top (SK 02964 55303, Passive Station) and Bradnop (SK 03842 54265)

These are two drive-by finds on the lane running NW from Waterhouses. Both are next to the road, only 1.3km apart. Moor Top is fitted with a plate showing that it is a Passive Station, part of the GPS system.

Bolehill East (SK 29386 55353)

Park in Middlepeak and take the Midshires Way NE to the edge of the Black Rock plantation. Then turn ESE and south along the public path to the pillar, returning by the lanes to the south.

Grindon Moor (SK 07153 55089)

This is another drive-by pillar, by the side of the lane running NW out of Grindon.

Martins Low (SK 07112 51986)

The pillar is next to a wall by the roadside. At best it makes a drive-by find, perhaps with Grindon Moor (above).

Hasker Farm (SK 26458 52516)

Ask at Hasker Farm itself; the pillar is just off the farm drive. There's a reasonable view over Carsington Water.

Alport Heights (SK 30560 51583, Primary)

The trigpoint is inside the boundary of one of the many mobile phone masts, but the spot is a widely walked National Trust area and it's possible to touch the pillar through the fence. On a clear day, the views extend to The Wrekin in Shropshire.

The Mountain (SK 26722 49270)

Walk south down the track from Kirk Ireton and use the GPS to establish when you are NW of the pillar. There is a stile and path towards the pillar, but the right of way stops short of a fence, with the pillar on the other side, and a clear 'Private' warning notice.

Ipstones (SK 01567 50069)

Park in Ipstones itself and make a short loop to the west. The pillar is close to the paths, with no issues about access.

Black Heath (SK 05021 49866)

This is best as a drive-by, maybe with Ipstones (above). The pillar is near a transmitter, against a stone wall, strictly on private land, but very close the lane.

Cliff Top (SK 13631 48153)

The pillar provides splendid views east over Dove Dale, but access is best from the west, parking off the A52 trunk road. It's private, so ask at Hillend Farm to the NW.

Also of Interest

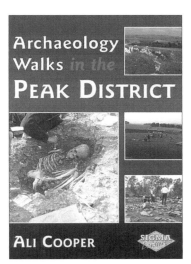

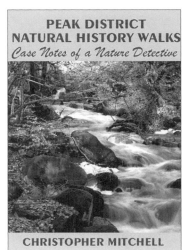

ARCHAEOLOGY WALKS IN THE PEAK DISTRICT

Ali Cooper

"... a new authoritative book ... for a spot of time travel while out walking" – *Derby Evening Telegraph*. These walks explore sites where there are visible features in the landscape: Bronze Age barrows, stone circles, caves, mines and much more. Walks are from 3 to 12 miles and are fully illustrated. Brief descriptions of the major finds are included, plus a bibliography for those who wish to delve deeper. *£7.95*

DARK PEAK HIKES:
off the beaten track

Doug Brown

The Dark Peak offers a dramatic landscape of steep slopes, gritstone crags and peat moorlands. Doug offers a collection of 34 challenging routes designed for those who enjoy the challenge of wandering 'off the beaten track', and using their navigational skills for route finding and locating items of interest: sites of aircraft wrecks; memorials; Bronze Age barrows; Iron Age forts; remnants of an industrial past; and even a New Age/UFO Society marker. *£7.95*

PEAK DISTRICT NATURAL HISTORY WALKS

Christopher Mitchell

A practical guide featuring 18 walks exploring the living landscape of this beautiful area. " ... a refreshingly-different walk guide which reads more like a Conan Doyle Sherlock Holmes novel, full of characters and sub-plots which the average walker would not even notice ..." – *from the Foreword by Roly Smith, President of the Outdoor Writers' Guild. £8.95*

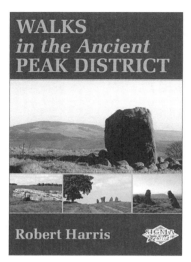

WALKS IN THE ANCIENT PEAK DISTRICT
Robert Harris

Here is a collection of walks visiting the prehistoric monuments and sites of the Peak District, including the White Peak, Dark Peak, Western and Eastern Moors. Explore rock shelters and caves of the old stone age, stone circles and burial chambers of the Neolithic and Bronze Ages and the great hill forts of the Iron Age. A refreshing insight into the thinking behind the monuments, the rituals and strange behaviour of our ancestors! *£8.95*

ROCKY RAMBLES IN THE PEAK DISTRICT:
Geology Beneath Your Feet
Fred Broadhurst

A walking guide with geological surprises at every turn – this is how to learn geology! What is seen along the way are not simply 'rocks' but materials that conceal fascinating facts relating to this part of the earth's crust – its minerals and fossils. Detailed maps are included plus parking and the all-important venues for refreshments. The comprehensive glossary of terms, which covers the identification of Peak District Rocks, forms an invaluable supplement providing 'at a glance' information for the reader. *£7.95*

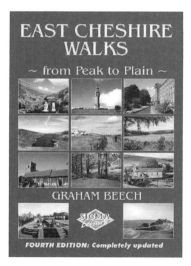

EAST CHESHIRE WALKS:
from Peak to Plain: 4th Edition
Graham Beech

The definitive guide to walking in East Cheshire is now in its fourth edition! Completely updated and revised, with nearly 40 walks (including one around the new runway!) covering 250 miles, there really is something for everyone. Footpath diversions fully documented. *£7.95*